Anatomy of an Actor

Meryl Streep

Karina Longworth

D1542829

Introduction

"Women are better at acting than men. Why? Because we have to be. If successfully convincing someone bigger than you are of something he doesn't know is a survival skill, this is how women have survived through the millennia. Pretending is not just play. Pretending is imagined possibility. Pretending or acting is a very valuable life skill, and we all do it. All the time."[1]
—Meryl Streep, 2010

Over the course of a forty-year career in film, television, and on the stage, Meryl Streep has earned nearly every accolade imaginable, including two Emmys, three Oscar wins, and seventeen nominations, the most of anyone in Academy history. Two of those wins, her best supporting actress for *Kramer vs. Kramer* (1979) and best actress for *Sophie's Choice* (1982), came within her first half decade of screen acting. Later, with films as disparate as *Silkwood* (1983) and *She-Devil* (1989), she helped to broaden the range of subjects and types of women depicted by major movie stars in mainstream productions. By taking sexualized roles in her forties (*The Bridges of Madison County* [1995]) and into her late fifties and early sixties (*Mamma Mia!* [2008], *It's Complicated* [2009]), she broke and thereby, to some extent, disproved film industry adages about what happens to actresses once they age out of the ingenue phase. She has maintained a high level of stardom for several decades while remaining grounded to something like normal experience, exemplified by her long-running marriage to artist Don Gummer and their brood of four children.

But before all of this—before Meryl Streep was *Meryl Streep*—her first "role" was the character she created for herself to survive high school. Mary Louise Streep, born on June 22, 1949, in middle-class, suburban Summit, New Jersey, was a gawky kid with glasses and frizzy hair. She took a directorial role in family home movies, parading her two younger brothers in front of the camera, with no thought of playing the ingenue herself. Then, at age twelve, she was chosen to sing at a school recital. Stunned to discover that their daughter had an excellent singing voice, her parents enrolled Meryl in opera lessons with the famed Estelle Liebling. Streep had talent, but she felt disconnected from opera. "I was singing

something I didn't feel and understand," she'd say later. "that was an important lesson—not to do that. To find the thing that I could feel through."[2] After four years, she quit Liebling's lessons to concentrate on being a teenager full-time. Wanting to join the cheerleading squad, Streep gave herself a makeover to look the part, bleaching and curling her hair to fit the mid-1960s ideal. But she soon learned that changing her physical appearance wasn't enough: her natural, outspoken personality was, in the teenage social scene, a liability. "Opinions," she'd recall, "were not, you know, attractive."[3]

At home, she was used to bickering with her two brothers, fighting to make her voice heard. "But I recognized early on that that wasn't attractive on a date. Like if he said something stupid and you go, 'No, I don't agree with that at all! That's—how can you say that? It's idiotic!' And that would not get a second date. So I would learn to go, '[giggle] Wow, yeah, cool,' you know. And that would be okay. So it's a form of acting for a purpose, which girls learned to do. And girls are good at it—if they care to be."[4] Teenage Streep didn't see this kind of performance as a precursor to an acting career—it was simply what she felt she had to do in order to get along.

By her senior year in high school, Streep had "actually convinced myself that I was this person and she, me. Pretty, talented, but not stuck-up. You know, a girl who laughed a lot at every stupid thing every boy said and who lowered her eyes at the right moment and deferred, who learned to defer when the boys took over the conversation. I really remember this so clearly, and I could tell it was working. I was much less annoying to the guys than I had been. They liked me better, and I liked that… This was real, real acting."[5]

"This Is So Ugly"

It's a decade after Streep's high school transformation. She's twenty-seven years old and she's never been in a movie, and now she's at a casting in Manhattan for the damsel role in the remake of *King Kong*. She's in front of legendary Italian producer Dino De Laurentiis. He's staring at her, and smiling, while berating his son Federico in Italian. "This is so ugly," he says. "Why did you bring me *this*?"

They think actresses are stupid, Streep thought. *They think Americans are stupid, too.*

Streep had studied Italian, for a year, at Vassar. In De Laurentiis's language, she said, "I'm very sorry that I'm not as beautiful as I should be but, you know—this is it. This is what you get." And she left. "I was very upset," she admitted later, "but I didn't show it."[6]

Streep knew she had broken the rules that a starlet is expected to follow, that she would now be labeled, by these producers and probably others, as "a pain in the ass." She didn't care. "I am a pain in the ass!" she exclaimed years later, remembering the incident. "How can I hide it? I mean, yeah, that is the package, you know, and… But I was not—I was not probably suited to that role, either. […] It represented something that […] I wasn't drawn to. So I suppose it was easier to be obstreperous in the meeting because of that."[7]

In owning up to being "a pain in the ass," even wearing that sobriquet as a badge of honor, Streep was taking a page from (almost directly quoting, in fact) the title character she played in Mike Nichols's *Silkwood* (1983), as well as a host of other roles throughout her career. She was drawn to playing, as she put it, "prissy women, disagreeable women, women whose motives are easily misconstrued […]."[8] At the same time, as a product of the social movements of the 1960s and 1970s, she understood that femininity was a performance, and as an unusually talented performer she could turn that performance on and off at will. The story of Meryl Streep's life and career is the story of a woman finding a working balance between her inherent "pain in the ass" nature, and an understanding, learned in adolescence, of the double standards to which ambitious, opinionated, powerful women are held. Hollywood, just like high school, would require her to carefully package her image in order to get along.

Role Playing

Streep began acting in movies at the end of the 1970s, entering the industry on the heels of enormous change in both Hollywood and America as a whole. The Vietnam War and the movement against it, the bubbling-up of second-wave feminism, the rise of a new generation of auteur filmmakers—the events of the decade fundamentally altered both attitudes and modes of being within American society and the ways in which American life was depicted on-screen. By the time she made the transition from stage acting to starring roles on-screen, Streep was in her late twenties; too old to play the part of impressionable ingenue on-screen or off, she was an adult woman with a formed worldview. That worldview was shaped by her experiences finding herself as a woman, and by female performers she worked with, admired, and/or measured herself against.

In 1967, Streep enrolled at Vassar, which was an all-female college when Streep arrived. As a freshwoman, she admitted later, "If you had asked me what feminism was, I would've thought it had something to do with having nice nails and clean hair."[9] For the first time she was living in an environment free of the pressures of the male gaze, and Streep soon felt empowered to drop the put-on passivity. "It was the classic consciousness-raising time. People really earnestly talking about, 'What's a woman? What's our role in the world? What's our capacity? What's holding us back?' All those things." Soon Streep "felt a thing emerge, which was my actual personality and my actual voice […] I realized that I was funny, and I was allowed to be. And I was allowed to be loud and obnoxious, and I took full advantage of it […]."[10] In 1969, the school went coed, and the entering male students brought with them a kind of activism that Streep later described as "bullshit": "I'm so sensitive to theater, and these boys would get up and perform. Everybody was a mini–Abbie Hoffman in front of this adoring swarm of girls."[11]

In high school she had starred in school plays, but she wasn't interested in serious theater, and claimed she never saw a nonmusical play until she starred in a Vassar production of *Miss Julie* in 1969. That production turned Streep into a campus star.

"I don't think anyone ever taught Meryl acting," said Vassar drama professor Clinton J. Atkinson. "She really taught herself."[12] She found she was naturally able to mimic accents and could memorize texts in a snap. "I'd read a script two or three times and I'd have my lines. The others were staying up at night studying their scripts." She added, "It's nothing I felt particularly good about, though."[13]

After graduation, she took a year off, performing with a small touring theater company. She applied for the Master's acting program at Yale because, she said, the application fee was cheaper than that of a similar program at Juilliard. She supported herself by waiting tables and typing on the side—even while performing in at least a dozen Yale productions a year. "[T]hey would post the cast lists of all the plays. I was always worried when the lists went up. Not because I was afraid I wasn't going to be on them. I was worried that I was going to be cast in the lead again. I was worried about how the rest of the class would feel about that."[14]

At Yale she worked so hard she got ulcers, and she contemplated quitting acting altogether, at one point applying for law school. Yale's program pulled Streep in multiple directions, exposing her to a wealth of varied and sometimes opposing techniques. "I had three different acting teachers for each of the three years," she said later. "But it was good, in a way, because you understood how he did it, and how he did it, and how she did it—

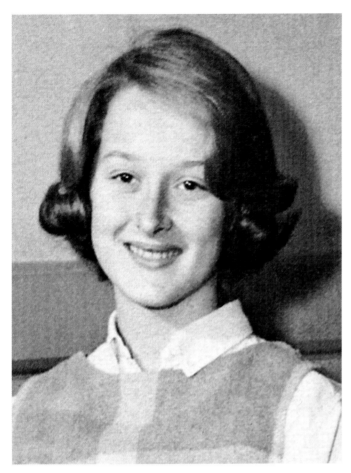

Meryl Streep and Jane Fonda
in *Julia* (1977), directed by
Fred Zinnemann.

Opposite: Streep as Karen
Traynor in Jerry Schatzberg's
The Seduction of Joe Tynan
(1979).

and [could] make up your own bag."[15] One of
those teachers was Robert Lewis, one of the
cofounders of the Actors Studio, which became
synonymous with Method acting and techniques
like emotional recall. At Yale, Streep bristled at
such exercises, feeling the professors "delved into
personal lives in a way I found obnoxious."[16]

In 1975, Streep arrived in New York, and
before even securing a place to live, she showed up
at an open audition at the Public Theater and was
cast by Joseph Papp in *Trelawny of the "Wells"*
alongside Mandy Patinkin and John Lithgow.
She played a total of six roles in her first year on
the New York stage. Papp then cast her in
Shakespeare in the Park productions of both
Henry V and *Measure for Measure*. On the latter,
Streep fell in love with her costar John Cazale;
the two would stay together until Cazale died
of cancer in 1978.

Streep wasn't angling for a film career, but she
was blown away by Robert De Niro's performance
in *Taxi Driver* (1976): "I said to myself, 'That's the
kind of actor I want to be when I grow up.'"[17]
In 1977, when she starred in *The Cherry Orchard*
and made her Broadway debut in *Happy End*,
Hollywood started to take notice. Spotted on
stage by casting director Juliet Taylor, Streep
landed her first film part, a small role in the Jane
Fonda vehicle *Julia* (1977). Most of her scenes
ended up on the cutting-room floor, and Streep
wasn't happy with the footage that was used in

the movie. "When I saw myself on screen for the
first time, I was horrified," she admitted.
"I had a bad wig and they took the words from
a scene I shot with Jane and put them in my
mouth in a different scene. I thought, I've made
a terrible mistake, no more movies. I hate this
business."[18] But one thing led to another, and
soon she was cast in the film that would change
her life: *The Deer Hunter* (1978). It was for that
film that in early 1979, less than four years after
she graduated from Yale's drama program,
Meryl Streep was nominated for her first Oscar.

Fonda, Minnelli, and Streep

Streep wasn't happy with *Julia*, but she spoke
glowingly about her first screen costar. "Jane was
so good to me. I hope I have enough sense to take
care of somebody the way she took care of me
then. I mean, she just literally saw how out to
lunch I was and took me by the arm."[19] One
wonders if Fonda was a role model for Streep off
set, too—a model of what not to do. Fonda's
political activism was such a major component of
her persona as a movie star that eventually it
overshadowed her work as an actress. Though
Streep considered herself a feminist and would
occasionally support liberal causes, she was wary
of publicly aligning herself with crusades,
particularly at the beginning of her career. Think
back to that lesson she learned as a teenage girl:

"Opinions are not attractive." Which is not to say that she didn't have them; instead of wearing her opinions on her sleeve the way Fonda did, Streep funneled them into her films without drawing attention to her own persona as an enlightened, liberated woman. "I admire Jane Fonda," Streep said in 1979. "But I also don't want to spend all my time immersing myself… in the business of myself…"[20]

If Jane Fonda was one of Streep's key formative influences, the other was, perhaps, less predictable: Liza Minnelli. Streep and Minnelli have never worked together, and they would appear on the surface to be two extremely different types of actresses and stars. But Streep has said repeatedly that Minnelli's 1977, Martin Scorsese-directed live show, *The Act*, sparked for her an acting epiphany. "I was sitting in the second balcony, and her desire to give you something was just so fantastic," Streep recalled later. "And I thought, 'That's an element you can't forget, in the private integrity of your work which makes everything real, *right in here*,'" she said, gesturing to her gut. "It's nice to open it," she added, spreading her arms, "and give it."[21] Minnelli made Streep understand that as much as realism and "truth-telling" were the core of character creation, "there is a further leap to the understanding of the importance of brilliance, sparkle and excitement. 'Performing' is the final gloss. It's a means to attract the audience to your character."[22]

How Does She Do It?

Streep has frequently asserted that her approach to acting is a whatever-works mishmash of the many styles and philosophies she learned in graduate school, a vague and nearly mystical process that she can't really articulate. "I have no method, you know," she said in 1987. "I've never read Stanislavski. I have a smattering of things I've learned from different teachers, but nothing I can put into a valise and open it up and say 'Now which one would you like?' Nothing I can count on and that makes it more dangerous. But then the danger makes it more exciting."[23]

She has proven herself to be extraordinarily gifted with accents, and she has made great use of external aids such as costuming, makeup, and physical objects. "[T]hat's my way in, the very beginning, how to enter," she confirmed in 2012. "Very quickly in the process, I don't think about the voice being separate from the way you hold your head, or the way you sit, or the way you put on lipstick. It's all a piece of a person, and it's all driven by conviction."[24]

Her performances are so external, and so chameleonic, that the "real" or essential Meryl can seem like a vague thing. She is an actress who impersonates characters, subsuming herself into them, rather than personifying them. "Once in a while," she admitted in 1988, "I think it would be a relief to play a housewife trying to raise three kids, keep her husband happy and organize her neighbors to fight pesticides." In other words, herself—and that she defines "herself" as a harried housewife is a sidelong way of acknowledging how hard she works to hide the real Meryl in exotic characters. She added, "I've always thought of acting as that disappearing act, always."[25]

The sleight-of-hand that Streep performs on-screen also tends to obscure her extraordinary involvement behind-the-scenes. Without ever receiving a writing or directing credit, Streep has unquestionably shaped her career and the roles within it as an auteur, breaking the mold of the actress as a passive vehicle for dialogue and direction by creating many characters, in whole or in part, through improvisation or by contributing her own dialogue. In fact, she thrives on hands-off direction, cherishing the freedom to play on set without interference. Her ideal director, she once said, "doesn't say anything to me… leaves me alone… [allows] you to make your mistakes and go as wild and as far out as you want."[26] And yet she has downplayed her involvement and level of control, often saying things like this: "I really don't get a choice; I don't produce my own movies. So, I'm sort of like the girl at the dance who waits to be asked."[27]

When she emerged out of the New York theater scene to star in four films in 1978 and 1979, Streep was compared to Jill Clayburgh and Diane Keaton, but she quickly stood on her own, in part because many of her first characters were so baldly unsympathetic: the adulterous lobbyist in *The Seduction of Joe Tynan* (1979), the mother who abandons her child in *Kramer vs. Kramer*, the memoir-publishing ex-wife in *Manhattan* (1979). Streep would later explain that she thought of herself as "a translator," tasked with "explaining people to each other, of being a conduit of mutual emotional understanding. I'm only being a little grandiose when I say I think that's why I've always been drawn to characters who are difficult to translate to other people, […] women who are hard to love."[28] It was a marked difference from female stars who represented everywomen or impossibly glamorous ideals.

She has seemingly worked hard off screen to promote an image of herself that's the complete opposite of the "disagreeable" but extraordinary women she often plays, selling the notion, as one article put it, that "the most extraordinary thing about Meryl Streep is her own ordinariness."[29] Long resistant to doing press at all, when Streep did give interviews, she artfully avoided revealing much about herself or her process, frequently stressing that her priority was her off-camera life as a housewife and mother of four children. She can be so incredibly modest about her own achievements that it sometimes seems like a put-on. "My achievement, if you can call it that, is that I've basically pretended to be extraordinary people my

Opposite: Streep thanks the
Academy for awarding her
an Oscar for her performance
in Alan J. Pakula's *Sophie's
Choice* (1982).

Meryl Streep in 1980.

entire life," Streep said in 2006, summing up
a thirty-year career that was by no means winding
down, "and now I'm being mistaken for one."[30]

Streep's public persona, based on downplaying
her talent, labor, and fame and playing up her
domestic life, serves as a distraction from—or
method to contain the threat of—the aspects of
her work and personal beliefs that challenge
patriarchal order and gender conventions. You
could say that she is and has always been that
teenage girl who learned that being demure was
the best way of getting along in a world in which
it's still controversial for women to be heard
rather than seen, and you could call this
regressive. Or you could say that because the
recessive act she learned as a teenage girl worked,
Meryl Streep very smartly used it as a weapon to
conquer the patriarchal industry of Hollywood,
and appeal to the largely conservative American
public, without appearing to be a ballbuster
or feather-ruffler. She has slyly infused nearly
every film she's made with some version of a
feminist point of view while selling herself as
a nonthreatening mom, as "just" a housewife
moonlighting as a movie star.

Ten Women

This book draws a portrait of Streep through
the analysis of ten screen performances, which
together suggest the essence and breadth of her
talent and accomplishment while also forming
an alternative, woman's history of the twentieth
century. The first half of the book considers
five disparate roles Streep played during the
first decade of her career. As Linda in *The Deer
Hunter* (Chapter 1), Streep counterbalanced an
exceedingly male view of the Vietnam War and
American life by embodying the girl next door
left behind. As the mother who leaves her husband
and son and then comes back for the latter in
Kramer vs. Kramer (Chapter 2), she movingly
spoke to the paradox of female experience as
second-wave feminism crashed into a climate of
increasing conservatism and corporate coldness.
The heartbreaking title heroine of *Sophie's Choice*
(Chapter 3) gave Streep her first opportunity to
deal directly with the role and perspective of
women in history, with the mentally and
emotionally fractured character's "choice"
speaking to a concern that Streep would return to
frequently throughout her career: the price women
pay for the political actions of men. With *Silkwood*
(Chapter 4) Streep for the first time played a real
person; as the story of political consciousness as
a process, it mirrored Streep's own increasing sense
of social responsibility. Finally, her career hit an
early peak with *Out of Africa* (1985, Chapter 5),
a best picture–winning blockbuster epic that gave
Streep the juicy role of a female adventurer while
also offering a muddled view of gender relations
that would hint at struggles soon to come.

The second half of the book considers Streep's uncommonly fertile middle age, which got off to a rocky start. When she turned forty in 1989, she said two decades later, "I remember turning to my husband and saying, 'Well, what should we do? Because it's over.'"[31] Streep attempted to skewer the challenges faced by aging women in Hollywood with *Death Becomes Her* (1992, Chapter 6), a moderate hit in a decade when it seemed like Streep couldn't get on the same wavelength as popular culture. Her only unequivocal success of this era was Clint Eastwood's *The Bridges of Madison County* (Chapter 7), in which Streep's rich performance is crucial to transforming what could have been a weak soap opera into a vibrant work of historical fiction implicitly critiquing postwar America's stifling culture of domesticity. Though Streep's fortunes began to turn around in 2002 with the one-two-three punch of *Adaptation*, *The Hours* (both released in 2002), and *Angels in America* (2003), it was playing the deliciously icy boss in 2006's *The Devil Wears Prada* (Chapter 8) that took her career to an unprecedented level. *Prada* was followed by a number of films in which the pushing-sixty Streep played a romantic lead, including *Julie & Julia* (2009, Chapter 9). With her fantasy caricature of Julia Child, Streep gave quite possibly the biggest performance of her career while also drawing on her own experience to bring lived-in truth to the story of a late bloomer. Finally, after nearly thirty years and a record-breaking seventeen nominations, Streep won her third Oscar for playing Margaret Thatcher in *The Iron Lady* (2011, Chapter 10). The Academy was perhaps not rewarding Streep for this broad, prosthetic-dependent performance on its own as much as they were quite belatedly giving a nod to the unmatched body of work behind her and her place within Hollywood history.

While she was promoting that film, history was very much on Streep's mind. In 2011, she became the public face of the drive to establish a National Women's History Museum on the Mall in Washington, DC. She was passionate about the project because, as she put it, "our history was written by the other team."[32]

As this book will argue, serving up a corrective to the patriarchal version of history has been the major project of Streep's acting career. Streep has not been extensively championed by feminists, perhaps because though she has often wielded creative power behind the scenes, she has also often been too good at playing the role of the girl "who lowered her eyes at the right moment and deferred"—refusing to take credit for being anything but a performer, frequently demurring when pressed to own her accomplishments. Some who have considered Streep's career from a feminist perspective have suggested that the productive, progressive elements of Streep's work have been canceled out by the way she sells herself, particularly her midcareer tendency to claim she was a mom and housewife first above all else, thus diminishing herself as an artist. As Karen Hollinger wrote in 2006, "When Streep, often portrayed as the greatest living Hollywood film actress, presents herself as a soccer mom who uses her career merely as a way to keep from becoming 'short' with her family, she demonstrates that she has so internalized established notions of traditional femininity that she herself initiates the cultural recuperation for patriarchy of her image as a strong, successful career woman."[33]

Since she was branded by the media as the "Star of the '80s," it's easy to see how Streep might have rankled feminists, who saw her as an icon for the culture's boomerang away from progressive conversations and change in the "backlash" decade. But if her success in raising four children and maintaining a marriage for thirty-plus years while remaining at or near the top of her field could be held up as an example that the feminist project was finished, the roles she chose and the way she played them spoke the truth to that lie. "None of her heroines are feminist, strictly speaking," wrote Molly Haskell, "yet they uncannily embody various crosscurrents of experience in the last twenty years, as women have redefined themselves against the background of the women's movement."[34] In playing and thereby giving voice to the voiceless, she has again and again authored alternative historical fiction, from a female point of view. That's more than speaking to feminism—that's enacting feminism.

Streep as Donna in Phyllida Lloyd's 2008 film adaptation of the musical *Mamma Mia!*

1

Linda

The Deer Hunter (1978)
Michael Cimino

"[Linda is] really far from my own instincts. I'm very much of a fighter myself. So this is very hard for me. I want to break her out of her straitjacket, but of course I can't even let that possibility show."[35]
—Meryl Streep, 1977

Meryl Streep took the role of Linda in Michael Cimino's *The Deer Hunter*—a vague, stock girlfriend part—because she was an exemplary girlfriend. Playing the spectral part of a woman defined by her relationships with two men would allow her to be near her own longtime boyfriend, John Cazale, who was acting in the film—and dying of cancer.

The path of domestic duty led to personal professional empowerment. *Hunter* functioned as a cinematic coming-out party for Streep, thanks to the phenomenal success of the film, and also because what she uniquely brought to it. Given free rein by Cimino to put words in the mouth of a sketchily drawn character, Streep turned Linda, a woman who the actress described as having been "forgotten" by both the men in her life and the writers of the screenplay, into the aching heart of the movie. She was rewarded for her efforts with the first Oscar nomination in a career that would come to be defined by quantity of nominations as much as the quality of her performances. An early landmark in the modern history of awards campaigning, the film's engineered dominance in that year's Oscar race perhaps benefited Streep more than any other performer. She was branded from the beginning of her movie career as an actress to be taken seriously.

Hunter's biggest Oscar rival was Hal Ashby's *Coming Home* (1978), starring Jane Fonda as a housewife whose antiwar activist awakening coincides with her sexual awakening. *Coming Home*'s hip, personal-is-political didacticism fit Fonda's personal brand; *Hunter* was an early bellwether of Streep's very different approach as a feminist actress. Where Fonda played the radical both on-screen and off in defiance of the mainstream, Streep made a case for female empowerment by playing a woman to whom empowerment was a foreign concept—a normal lady from an average American small town, for whom subservience was the only thing

she knew—within a film that amounted to a rallying cry for the kinds of conservative attitudes that Fonda had spent years striking against. Streep, in making the pain and frustration of powerless women real and visible in a vehicle that otherwise spoke to an increasingly conservative public, critiqued the mainstream while participating in it—an act of subversion that passed as submission.

A Girl Between the Guys

The Deer Hunter was initiated by British producer Michael Deeley, who purchased a script about Vietnam vets and Russian roulette in 1976 and shopped it around town; every studio turned it down. "The consensus," according to Deeley, "was that American audiences would have no stomach or savour for a picture concerning the Vietnam War."[36]

In need of a writer-director to revise the script, Deeley settled on Michael Cimino, who had written *Silent Running* (1972) and two pictures for Clint Eastwood, *Magnum Force* (1973) and *Thunderbolt and Lightfoot* (1974). Deeley used Cimino's new script to lure Robert De Niro for the lead role of Michael, the Pennsylvania coal miner who heads to Vietnam with two friends and watches the war destroy them, while he emerges physically unscathed but emotionally changed. With De Niro locked in, studios, sniffing accolades in the air, put aside their objections to the material. Deeley set the film up at Universal, which was hungry for prestige. "The studio hadn't won a Best Picture Oscar for decades but head of production Ned Tanen wanted to engage in something more serious," Deeley wrote. "*The Deer Hunter*'s script was certainly that."[37]

De Niro lured Christopher Walken to play Nick, and John Cazale—Fredo in the *Godfather* movies—to play Stan, a sleazy hunting buddy. After seeing Cazale's girlfriend, Meryl Streep, on Broadway, De Niro recommended her for the part of Linda, Nick's girlfriend who is left behind when the men go off to war.

"I was in *The Cherry Orchard*, where I played a maid who fell down every time she came on and just before she left the stage—for laughs, clearly. [De Niro] saw something in me that he thought would be good for Linda in

Meryl Streep on the set of Michael Cimino's *The Deer Hunter* (1978).

Top: Michael Cimino cast
Streep to play Linda on the
advice of Robert De Niro,
who was convinced of her
talent after seeing her in
a Broadway production.

Bottom: Nick does not come
home from Vietnam. Here,
Axel (Chuck Aspegren),
Michael (Robert De Niro),
Stan (John Cazale), and John
(George Dzundza) carry
his coffin.

The Deer Hunter, which speaks to his great imagination," Streep remembered with a laugh.[38]

Describing what it was that he saw in Streep, De Niro gave his costar a kind of backhanded compliment. "Women who are very beautiful often let their beauty inhibit them. They tend to have no character. When a woman is beautiful and has an extra edge—like Meryl—it's nice."[39]

Streep was rather agnostic about movie acting. After just two years on Broadway, she was already a big fish in the New York theater world and was in no hurry to interrupt that thriving career to jump into the very different world of film acting, which required a different skill set, one she was anxious she didn't have. And the role of Linda did not jump out at her as a part she was uniquely suited to play; as one reporter put it, "It concerns Streep that [Linda] is one of 'those blond-haired woman parts,' the kind of part she has tried to sidestep on stage."[40] But Cazale wasn't getting better, and the film would allow her to spend valuable time with him.

Cazale's illness was initially kept secret, so as to not alarm Universal; Cimino scheduled to shoot Cazale's scenes first, to minimize the time he needed to spend on location. But the secrecy couldn't last long, and when the suits discovered one of the film's stars was dying, they demanded Cimino recast the role. In protest, Streep declared that if Cazale was fired, she would leave the project, too. Eventually De Niro put up his own money to secure Cazale's insurance. He completed the shoot, and died five months after he wrapped, nine months before the movie was released. He was forty-two, and Streep was twenty-eight.

Streep was happy to take the part, she said, "because I was living with John Cazale at the time and we could be in it together." She was under no illusions about the heft of the role. "They needed a girl between the two guys, and I was it."[41]

The Forgotten Woman

A three-act, nearly three-hour epic, *The Deer Hunter* begins and ends in a small Pennsylvania town dominated by the steel industry. The film focuses on a group of men who work, drink, and hunt deer together. De Niro's Michael believes the essence of the hunt is to kill a deer in "one shot… two is pussy." Michael, Christopher Walken's Nick, and John Savage's Steven are drafted and sent to Vietnam while others (including Cazale's Stanley) stay behind.

In Vietnam, Michael, Nick, and Steven end up in a POW camp, forced by the sadistic Viet Cong to play Russian roulette. Michael devises a scheme: they'll escape by convincing their captors to let him and Nick play the deadly game against each other, and then shoot their way out. It works, but in flight the three men are forced to go their separate ways. Disoriented at a veterans' hospital, Nick starts to call Linda, but can't do it; he soon

thereafter falls into the Saigon underworld. Michael returns home alone and begins a tentative relationship with Linda, who hasn't heard from Nick once since he's been away. Michael then discovers that Steven is living in a local rehab facility—he lost both of his legs during their escape—and has been receiving mysterious bundles of money from someone in Vietnam. Convinced Nick is the benefactor, Michael goes back to Saigon to try to bring him home. He finds his old friend in an underground gambling parlor, playing Russian roulette for money. Transformed by trauma and looking drugged out, Nick doesn't immediately recognize Michael, but then it clicks. "One shot," Nick says, then raises the gun to his temple, fires, and blows himself away. The film ends back in Pennsylvania, with Michael, Linda, and the others gathered for Nick's wake, where the friends spontaneously sing a chorus of "God Bless America."

In *The Deer Hunter*, men are warrior heroes whose every activity is fully engaged with the tension between life and death. Women function as ghosts on their periphery. Cimino has claimed that he didn't set out to make a film about Vietnam specifically, but was instead interested in war in general as a rite of passage adventure in the lives of young men, its function as a break from small-town monotony—and, by implication, small-town girls—by seeing the world and testing themselves through foreign experience. But his portrait of men at war valorized the American soldiers and demonized the Vietnamese in a way that felt to some like a whitewashing of the war and its outcome. Many film critics, cultural commentators, antiwar activists, and veterans protested the film on the grounds that the Vietnamese were made out to be cartoonish villains to the American's superheroes.

To the extent that *The Deer Hunter* has a credibly humanist message, Cimino's slow study of the men in blissfully ignorant homeland machismo is crucial to it. These are not fresh-faced suburban college boys forced to go to war against their will; their work is dangerous, their hobby is killing. They are the type who should be well equipped for military service, but to a man, they are painfully battle scarred. The film evokes a version of dominant masculinity in which male friendship is a powerful force, greater than romantic relationships with women, and then reveals the tragedy and desperation of such a life for all involved. As the only significant female presence in the film, Streep becomes the film's coal mine canary: from start to finish, she represents the collateral suffering left in the wake of unchecked, hyper-masculinity.

The film's tendency to overlook Linda was key to Streep's conception of the character. "I wanted the audience to feel another dimension in her," Streep noted. "She's the forgotten

Opposite: In her second film role, Streep played Linda, a young woman of humble origin defined by shyness, a certain enthusiasm, and anguish.

At their wedding, Steven (John Savage) and Angela (Rutanya Alda) are surrounded by their friends. To the left are Michael, Axel, Stan, Axel's girlfriend (Mady Kaplan), and a bridesmaid (Amy Wright); Linda is on the right.

Following pages: With no news about Nick, Linda grows closer to Michael, who is back from Vietnam.

person in the screenplay and also in the other characters' lives."[42]

Streep's first scene positions Linda as a martyr for all females unlucky enough to get stuck in such a town. Wearing a cream puff of a bridesmaid dress, Linda attempts to feed her father before leaving for Steven's wedding. Linda enters his bedroom and finds her father slumped against a wall, dangerously deep into a drinking jag, babbling incoherently.

"Fuckin' bitch!" Dad exclaims as she's helping him onto his bed. He reaches back and slaps her with the back of his hand, so hard she falls to the floor. Linda takes a minute to regain her composure and turns to her father, smiling, to see that he is still angry and apparently intent on punishing his daughter for the sins of all women. "I hate 'em," he says, raising his hand as she stands up. Linda cries out, "Daddy, no, it's me!" He responds with another slap. "Fuckin' bitches!" He finally collapses on his bed, out of breath. She sobs quietly, so softly that you can hear a clock ticking in the room—an unsubtle signal that time is running out for her.

With a ratty fur draped over her shoulders, Linda trudges through an overgrown lot, dragging a suitcase up to the trailer shared by Nick and Michael. Nick meets her out front, surprised to see her, and asks her what's the matter. She mumbles a barely audible, "He hit me." She asks Nick if she could move into the

trailer once he and Michael leave for Vietnam. Though still sniffling back tears, she makes the request very formally, her arms folded over her chest, acting like it's a business transaction—she even insists on paying rent. Nick takes her face in his hands and reminds her, "It's me you're talking to." She laughs through her tears.

Streep's Linda exudes shy, girlish enthusiasm and world-weary anxiety simultaneously. She has a slight accent, a softening of consonants indicating geography as well as a lack of education. She's so conciliatory that she sometimes seems not all there, mentally and morally. When Nick spontaneously proposes, she drops her jaw and blurts out her answer: "Yeah!" When Michael returns from the war, alone, she welcomes him into her life incredibly eagerly.

"I thought to myself: *Oh, boyyyy, how am I gonna stand up for this character?*" Streep admitted. "I thought of all the girls in my high school who waited for things to happen to them. Linda waits for a man to come and take care of her. If not this man, then another man: she waits for a man to make her life happen."[43]

Cimino doesn't show Nick or Michael even saying good-bye to Linda—after the wedding, the men hunt and drink together, and then Cimino cuts to Vietnam—signaling that she's out of mind even before she's out of sight. When the film returns to Pennsylvania, at first Linda is desperately thankful for any attention at all.

In 1977, after wrapping her work on *The Deer Hunter*, Meryl Streep traveled to Austria to star in *Holocaust*, a television miniseries in which she played the Christian wife of a German-Jewish painter (played by James Woods) who is sent to a concentration camp. The material was even less impressive to Streep than the male-dominated film she had just finished. "I did it for the money," she admitted. "I needed it very badly, and I make no bones about that."[a]

In addition to her graduate school debt, Streep was paying John Cazale's medical bills. Perhaps the most frustrating aspect of the *Holocaust* experience was that as the over-schedule production dragged on, Cazale's cancer was worsening. When Streep finally returned to New York after four months, she moved into Cazale's hospital room, and was constantly by his side until the day he died, March 12, 1978. *Holocaust* aired on US television in April 1978, months before *The Deer Hunter* was released. Streep's notoriety increased instantly. One day when Streep was riding her bike in Manhattan, she recalled, "these four guys in a Volkswagen started yelling at me out of the window, 'Hey, *Holocaust*, hey, *Holocaust*!' Can you imagine? It's absurd that that episode in history can be reduced to people screaming out of car windows at an actress."[b] *Holocaust* netted Streep the Emmy Award for Outstanding Actress in a Miniseries or Television Movie, but she declined to attend the ceremony. "I don't believe performances should be taken out of context and put up against each other for awards,"[c] she said in an interview published in February 1979. Just over a year later, she would accept her first Oscar, for *Kramer vs. Kramer*—an early landmark in a career renowned in part for attracting the most Academy Award nods in movie history.

Opposite: Streep as Inga
Helms Weiss in *Holocaust*
(1978), a miniseries directed
by Marvin J. Chomsky.

Streep and De Niro on the set.
They've shared the screen
only twice, in *The Deer Hunter*
and in *Falling in Love* (1984).

On their first reunion, Michael asks how she is, and she seems surprised to be asked. "Uh, me?" She laughs. "I'm okay. I'm fine. I go along, you know." When he then asks if he can walk her to work, she looks at him in disbelief, shaking her head, trying to find the words. Finally, she blurts out, "I'm so glad you're alive!" She embraces him, then admits, "I really don't know what I feel." Perhaps deciding what to feel has never been an option for her.

Slowly, Linda gathers the courage to ask for what she wants. She propositions Michael: "Why don't we go to bed? Can't we just comfort each other?" He declines, but she follows him to a motel. "Comfort" indeed seems to be the thrust of the relationship that ensues. In contrast to the carnal depiction of life after war in *Coming Home*, the Michael and Linda affair is depicted as tender and innocent, nearly chaste, the coming together of two horribly broken people with no one else to turn to.

The relationship doesn't fill the hole in either of their lives. Michael's return to Vietnam suggests that Nick is his truer love than Linda (indeed, many have noted that Linda functions as a conduit for Nick and Michael's barely repressed feelings for each other). And in the film's final scene, without spoken dialogue, Streep gives an indication that Linda has been changed by her experiences. Just before the wake scene devolves into the questionably ironic choral show of patriotism, there's a close-up on Linda, staring at Michael. Her eyes seem to be full of the anger and frustration that she hasn't dared let come to the surface previously.

Streep would note years later, with no small amusement, that President Bill Clinton had told her Linda was his favorite among her roles. "I have my own secret understanding of why that is, and it confirms every decision I made in high school," Streep said. Linda, she felt, "was just behaving in a way that cowed girls, submissive girls, beaten up girls with very few ways out have behaved forever and still do in many worlds."[44]

The Deer Hunter may primarily be a film about men losing themselves, but with Streep in the female lead, it can also be read as a film in which a woman, for the first time in her life, figures out what she wants. By the final frames of the film, Streep has wrested control of a stock girlfriend character and turned her into a human being with a point of view. That in itself was a feminist revision.

Learning Curve

Streep's accomplishment in this, her first major role, was significant, and it wasn't easy. For starters, she was inexperienced acting in front of a camera, and the process wearied her. "The camera takes everything out of you," she said. "If you're not real, it takes that too."[45]

At the time, Streep was living with John Cazale. She accepted the role of Linda so she could be as close as possible to her partner, who was suffering from cancer and died a few months later.

Opposite: At first Streep wasn't sure she brought anything to the role of Linda. However, she would do much to enhance a character that was somewhat neglected by the filmmakers.

Following pages: The actress and the film's director, Michael Cimino.

Her friend Joe Grifasi, who appeared in a bit part in *The Deer Hunter*, remembers Streep "would come up to me at the end of the day and say, 'How can you enjoy this?'"[46]

Streep and Cazale "would talk about the process endlessly, and he was monomaniacal about the work," Streep remembered later. "I think probably I was more glib, and ready to pick the first idea that came to me. And he would say to me, 'There's a lot of other possibilities.' And that was a real lesson. I really took that to heart, and I always think about it." She was inspired, too, by Cazale's own approach, "the responsibility he felt to a fictional character, as though it were a real soul."[47]

But the script gave her little to work with. The filmmakers, she said, "admitted they didn't have any idea what the girl would say in any of these situations—just whatever I thought would be appropriate. On the one hand you could think of it as negligent. On the other, it was great artistic freedom for me because I could really do my performance."[48] What the script did give her contradicted Streep's own philosophy. "Linda is essentially a man's view of a woman," Streep said during the shoot. "She's extremely passive, she's very quiet, she's someone who's constantly vulnerable."[49]

She echoed those sentiments in the film's official press notes—and, if anything, was even more unsparing in her assessment. "I wouldn't exactly call this a strong woman's part," she sniffed. "The fact is this is a man's story and my character is called upon to be there—strong and supportive for the men. That concept is not anywhere close to my personal values." That seems like a startling admission for a young, up-and-coming actress to make in the context of a film's official promotional material. Perhaps to lessen the blow, Streep followed it up with a more typical starlet's show of gratitude: "But don't get me wrong, working with such fine actors as Robert De Niro and others in the film was just wonderful."[50]

Was Streep speaking out of turn? Or, by publishing Streep's comments which drew a distinction between her own liberated vision of womanhood and that of the character she played (who is defined entirely by her relationships with and proximity to men), was Universal's press department savvily framing Streep's performance as a break from the actress's own character, which made her work seem more challenging and impressive? Maybe allowing the actress to speak unguardedly was the first step in selling her persona as the consummate modern actress.

An Early Oscar Marketing Triumph

Filmed in 1977, *The Deer Hunter* was not released until December 1978, in part because the studio had no idea what to do with it. An early test screening in Detroit was, as Universal's Thom

Mount remembered, "the worst preview I'd ever seen."[51] Nervous about how to market the film even after Cimino made cuts, Universal called on marketing guru Allan Carr. The film was going to have to play in Los Angeles for at least one week before the end of 1978 in order to be eligible for 1979's Oscar ceremony. Carr declared that Universal should also open the film temporarily in New York to create a buzz and qualify for local critics' awards—and then take the film out of theaters until the Oscar nominations were revealed in early 1979.

It worked—*The Deer Hunter* was nominated for nine Academy Awards. Streep, the only actress with significant screen time in the movie, was caught up in the wave, earning her first Oscar nomination. Though she lost (to Maggie Smith, for *California Suite* [1978]), the film's many wins, including best picture, validated Carr's unique strategy. *The Deer Hunter* had become the zeitgeist movie of the year. Some people loved it, others hated it, but everyone had an opinion.

Critics generally gave Streep credit for pulling a magic trick, especially considering how little she apparently had to work with. Negative reviews singled her out as the film's saving grace. Calling her a "real beauty," Pauline Kael noted that Streep "doesn't do anything standard; everything seems fresh. But her role is to be the supportive woman, who suffers and endures, and it's a testament to Meryl Streep's heroic resources as a mime that she makes herself felt—she has practically no lines."[52] It's notable that Kael, who would in time become one of Streep's fiercest critics, found space in her pan of *The Deer Hunter* to praise Streep even while eviscerating the way her character was used.

For his part, Cimino insisted that anyone who "criticized the fact [Linda] wasn't very independent"—presumably, his actress included—was misreading the film. Writing off such critics as hopelessly "petit bourgeois," Cimino added, "They wouldn't recognize a real worker if he popped out of their toasters. That a girl like her, in a small town like that, where everyone knows everyone, where everyone knows what you do, where everyone talks about it, would leave her father's to go live, in a trailer, with those two guys, and stay after only one of them returns! That shows that she is a character with a very strong will; one must be very strong to act thusly, in a community like that, where religion plays a very important role."[53]

On Oscar night, a group called Vietnam Veterans Against the War protested on the street in front of the ceremony. Thirteen were arrested in a clash with police. In the press room, Cimino said he was "puzzled by those demonstrating."[54] Fonda, who won best actress for *Coming Home*, spoke to the press next, and before answering questions about her own victory, she weighed in on the *Deer Hunter* controversy. "I know many of those people out there protesting. They're friends of mine," Fonda said. "They know a lot about Vietnam and feel *The Deer Hunter* delivers a Pentagon view of the Vietnamese. *The Deer Hunter* just does not help us learn the lessons of the Vietnam war."[55]

Fonda, who had conceived *Coming Home* and hired Nancy Dowd to write the story, was livid that her film had lost best picture—and, arguably, the fight for the zeitgeist—to a movie that she felt kicked mud in the face of her own activism. (Fonda later admitted that she had never seen *The Deer Hunter*.) Fonda was not the only one taking sides; those who defended *The Deer Hunter* often disparaged *Coming Home* and vice versa. As critic David Denby wrote in an essay on the *Hunter* backlash, "I refuse to take that guilty-liberal erotic fantasy, *Coming Home*, very seriously."[56]

Streep's criticism of Linda's character stopped short of attacking the film politically. Her own experience of Vietnam was limited to having had a boyfriend who had fought there and come back a heroin addict. "My consciousness was I didn't want him to go. It was just a personal thing. I was against the war like everybody else, but I wasn't very political."[57] This put Streep in sharp contrast to the flagrantly outspoken Fonda. Streep's on-screen approach to making the lives and experiences of real women visible would continue along such subtly subversive lines. In *Kramer vs. Kramer*, released just twelve months after *The Deer Hunter*, Streep played another women whose life had been defined by her subservience to men. Both films used that female character as a way to acknowledge the collateral damage patriarchy inflicts on powerless women. But unlike the "weak" Linda, Joanna Kramer would actually attempt to radically challenge the role she was assigned in that society, to stand up for the right to determine her own course in life. Joanna would suffer the consequences; Streep would win the Oscar.

After the funeral, the group of friends gather to honor Nick's memory. An exchange of glances between Linda and Michael in this scene speaks volumes.

2

Joanna Kramer

Kramer vs. Kramer (1979)
Robert Benton

"In 1979, nobody was talking about depression, but [Joanna Kramer] probably thought about killing herself once or twice a day. I could understand the compulsion to leave and not want take your little boy wherever you were going to get better. I didn't think she was horrible [...] I was on her side."[58]
—Meryl Streep, 2000

The Ambivalent Feminist

Streep couldn't have chosen a better showcase for her first prominent role than *The Deer Hunter*, whose dominance of American culture circa 1979 culminated in its best picture win. But the victory of the film, and the enormous attention it brought to Streep, was bittersweet given the loss of John Cazale. She coped with her grief by throwing herself into work.

Immediately after Cazale's death, Streep signed on to play Alan Alda's seducer in Jerry Schatzberg's *The Seduction of Joe Tynan*. She took a small role in *Manhattan*. And then, she took a meeting with producer Stanley Jaffe, writer/director Robert Benton, and actor Dustin Hoffman. The trio were in the process of making a movie based on *Kramer vs. Kramer*, Avery Corman's hit 1977 novel in which a workaholic and his young son bond when their wife/mother walks out on them—and then comes back, seeking custody of her son. They needed an actress to play Joanna, the unhappy housewife whose self-interest (or self-preservation) tears the family apart. Joanna was not the book's most sympathetic character—*Ms.* magazine disparaged Corman's *Kramer vs. Kramer* as an "antifeminist backlash novel," citing a "woman-hating element in the book's success"[59]—and Streep was not the first choice for the role. In June 1978, Kate Jackson from television's *Charlie's Angels* (1976–1981, though Jackson left in 1979) came to Manhattan to read for the part and spent a day with Hoffman that, according to gossip columns, ended with a night at Studio 54. But Jackson couldn't get out of her TV schedule, opening the door for, and perhaps emboldening, Streep. Cazale had taught her to ask questions, to find out where the filmmaker was coming from in order to best serve the material. When she met with the *Kramer* team, she didn't shy away from questioning these filmmakers or the material itself.

The problem with Joanna, in Streep's mind, was that she was too one-dimensional, her troubles were not taken seriously, she was too facilely positioned as a villain. Streep felt Joanna's struggles within the role of homemaker, the desperation that leads her to abandon her family in order to "find" herself, reflected real tensions in real American lives. To close the audience off to Joanna's point of view would be to close the film off from the many women who also struggled to define themselves in the conflicting spheres of work and family, who felt torn between traditional roles and responsibilities and the widening of possibilities, practical and theoretical, made possible by the social movements of the previous decade. And these weren't issues specific to Streep's generation—her own mother had told her, "All my friends at one point or another wanted to throw up their hands and leave and see if there was another way of doing their lives."[60]

"The more I thought about it, the more I felt the sensual reason for Joanna's leaving, the emotional reasons, the ones that aren't attached to logic," Streep would say. "Joanna's daddy took care of her. Then Ted took care of her. Suddenly she just felt incapable of taking care of herself. I wanted to play a woman who had this feeling of incapability, because I've always felt that I can do anything."[61]

The all-male team behind *Kramer vs. Kramer* felt the actress had a point. Streep was cast, and the script was rewritten to reflect her suggestions. Insisting on the reformulation of her character was an incredibly bold move for an actress in her first flush of movie stardom; that the gambit succeeded suggests the extraordinarily high esteem in which Streep was already held. She was savvily standing up for what she believed in behind the scenes, but was careful about the way she branded herself in the media. In December 1979, *People* magazine asked Meryl Streep if she was a feminist.

"Yeah, sure," she said with a shrug. "Why not?"[62]

Turning a Villain Around

For producer Jaffe, the character of Ted Kramer was "really a kind of hero." Ted's estranged wife was more complicated: "One of the real problems in telling this story is to understand the motivation

In Robert Benton's *Kramer vs. Kramer* (1979), Streep plays a woman who leaves her child and husband in order to find new meaning in her life.

35

of Joanna Kramer."[63] That was a problem that fell to Streep to solve, just as it had fallen to her to add shading to Linda.

"A lot of what the other characters do and say has to do with me, but I'm really only there at the beginning and at the end [of the movie]," Streep noted. "It's like a person who walks out of the room, and everybody tries to explain why she did what she did, and finally, after they've agreed on some versions of things, she comes back and explains herself. I'm set up as a villain, so I like the idea of reappearing and trying to turn that around."[64]

Streep appears in Kramer's first image and delivers the film's first line of dialogue, saying good-bye to her six-year-old son. When Ted Kramer returns to the family apartment after a late night at work, his wife coolly announces that she's leaving, handing over her keys and a receipt for dry cleaning as though that's all it takes to untangle a decade of marriage. "It's me, it's my fault," she insists. He tries to drag her back into the apartment, and she gasps, "Please don't make me go in there," as though their marital home is a torture chamber. She makes it to the elevator. "And I don't love you anymore." The elevator doors close. She's gone, her packed suitcase left behind in the apartment.

The husband left behind is hurt, but more than that, angry. How could Joanna leave so suddenly, knowing that having to suddenly assume full care of their son would really cramp Ted's corporate go-getter style? He suggests that Margaret (Jane Alexander), a divorcée friend of Joanna's, put his wife up to this. "It took a lot of courage for her to walk out of here," Margaret says. Ted fires back: "How much courage does it take to walk out on your kid?"

This exchange is emblematic of the "antifeminist backlash" perspective that the film sometimes supports. Ted's point of view is that it's a man's job to do whatever it takes outside of the home to pay for the home, which he can do only if the woman holds up her part of the bargain: to run the home. The role Ted is asking his wife to play is both supporting and background. It's depersonalized, having nothing to do with the person she actually is (she tells Ted he "married the wrong woman" for the job), and Ted's inability to see that and reverse course has dehumanized her.

Once Joanna departs, Kramer assumes Ted's point of view. The character, and the film, are initially hard and hostile toward the estranged wife; that perspective ultimately softens enough to allow her side to make an emotional impression, if not to fully counteract his moral position. Ted's transformation, and the film's, is reflected by the change in the way he speaks of Joanna in two scenes bookending the film's first half.

The morning after Joanna leaves, Ted arrives at work and confides his domestic problems to his boss. Of Joanna, he admits, "I've known when she was upset, because she gets very quiet," but again he insists all would've been fine if not for their divorcée neighbor. "She's got this friend Margaret downstairs and…"—Ted makes a chattering sound and gesture—"women's lib…" He trails off, and his boss laughs in recognition, as though wanting to be treated like a human being is a silly phase all modern wives go through. Though Ted is still clearly wedded to his career, this scene begins to suggest that his work environment is toxic, and that it will become necessary for him to take his foot off the professional gas pedal for the good of his family, when his boss suggests that Ted send Billy (Justin Henry) to live with a relative so Ted can concentrate on work "twenty-four hours a day." The dehumanization that Joanna was experiencing in a marriage that chained her to the home is a mirror to what's happening to Ted in the workplace: what he wants and needs outside of that machine does not matter. To Streep, Ted was "the prototypical 70s person […] when you see the way he has to behave to make a living, it's horrible."[65]

Later Ted articulates his understanding that his single-minded pursuit of career deprived Joanna and pushed her out the door. "I think the reason why Mommy left was because, for a long time now, I've kept trying to make her be a certain kind of person, Billy," he explains to his distraught son. "A certain kind of wife that I thought she was supposed to be. And she just wasn't like that. She was… she just wasn't like *that*. And now that I think about it, I think that she tried for so long to make me happy. And when she couldn't, she tried to talk to me about it, see? But I wasn't listening because I was too busy or I was too wrapped up just thinking about myself."

This confession is endearing—it gives the impression that Ted now understands the error of his ways and feels remorse for his part in driving his ex-wife to do the unthinkable in abandoning her son. Thus, without the actress appearing on-screen, Streep's character has evolved from villain to victim. But when Joanna returns, it becomes apparent that Ted—and the film—are a long way off from fully understanding Joanna's point of view. It becomes Streep's task to turn this spectral presence, who has structured the film with her absence, into a human being.

Oil and Water

Eighteen months after her departure, Joanna returns and, over drinks, announces to Ted that she's "learned a great deal" about herself and has realized, "I love my little boy, and that I'm capable of taking care of him." In short: "I want my son." To which Ted responds, "You can't have him."

The end of their exchange seems to hint at what was so wrong in their home that she needed to take drastic steps in order to assert herself.

Director Richard Benton with his two principal actors, Dustin Hoffman and Meryl Streep, during the making of the film.

Following pages: Ted Kramer (Hoffman) tries to convince his wife, Joanna, not to leave their marital home.

After several months, Joanna returns to New York to try to explain her actions. She's learned a lot about herself and asks for custody of her son. Ted categorically refuses.

As Joanna attempts to calmly state her case, Ted stands up, mutters, "You do what you have to do." His parting gesture is to strike his hand through his wineglass, flinging it against the wall next to her head. Streep brings her hands up to her mouth reflexively, her eyes filled with a particular kind of fear. As when Streep's Linda was hit by her father, here the actress conveys that the character is scared not because this act of violence is so unexpected, but because she knows this man all too well and has been the target of his anger before. When that wineglass smashes against the wall, with it smashes any illusion that Ted has really changed, that he's learned how to compromise his own needs to make room for someone else.

The friction between these two characters is the product of a friction between two actors with radically different styles. Streep did not remember their first encounter fondly. Years before shooting the film, she auditioned for a play Hoffman was directing. "He came up to me and said, 'I'm Dustin—burp—Hoffman,' and he put his hand on my breast. What an obnoxious pig, I thought."[66]

Hoffman, twelve years Streep's senior, was an Actors Studio–trained perfectionist. He lived his roles. *Kramer* hit particularly close to home: at the time of the shoot, Hoffman was estranged from his own wife of ten years, Anne Byrne, who left her career as a dancer when they married but eventually became restless in the marriage and went back to work. Hoffman's on-set style was aggressive; he had ideas about everything and insisted that they be heard.

Streep was still developing her style, still struggling to act in front of a camera. "I'd feel less insecure if I had a method when I was working," she admitted. "Instead, I approach everything I do in a different way. When I was at Yale I wanted some tools, something I could get my hands on in this ephemeral art. I learned that the only thing you can count on is that you can't count on anything."[67] On *Kramer*, she said, "I was lucky because Benton worked like a theatrical director. He saw the film as a collaboration of talents, whereas most movie directors don't look at it as a collaboration of anything. They're afraid of relinquishing control of the project. They see it as a threat."[68] She was naïve enough, she said later, to think "that was the way people made films. And later on I realized, no. They want you to shut the fuck up. The talent. Put the clothes on and say what you're supposed to say."[69]

Her research on *Kramer* consisted of hanging around playgrounds in Manhattan, watching moms watching their children, and shopping and lunching. These women, Streep would later say, "had a stillness that seemed suffocating. Here they are with everything they ever dreamed of, but they are alone. They're not happy and they don't know why."[70] She also read magazines geared toward mothers her age. "Every month, they carried the same story," Streep marveled. "'Judge Mary So-and-So, brilliant jurist and mother of five, handles her career and this amazing household, together, terrific!' Everything this woman reads tells her that she must be able to do both! But what if you can't do both? What if you just can't handle it? What if you can't understand why the world won't allow you to do one or the other?"[71] Streep's own sympathy for this balancing act would become crucial to the character, as she fought to make Joanna less of a device, the binary opposition to Ted, and more of a living person.

Hoffman and Streep had their biggest on-set conflict over the scene in which Joanna returns and announces that she wants custody of Billy. As the scene was originally written, Joanna revealed her intentions at the beginning of the meeting. Streep argued that, instead, she should lead her ex-husband on a bit, make him feel comfortable before she admits the purpose behind her return. Streep won the battle—the scene in the finished film is all the more effective because Hoffman so clearly feels betrayed that his ex-wife tried to sweet-talk him into relinquishing control over their son—but Hoffman and Streep's squabble became the stuff of movie legend. Years later, when a journalist asked Streep about the incident, he suggested that Hoffman "wanted to kill you."

"He didn't mean that," Streep responded. "He meant it in one scene. [...] In the end he agreed with me. But with him everything is a competition, that's what gets his juices going: who's winning. And in that piece, that was appropriate."[72]

"I hated her guts," Hoffman admitted. "But I respected her. She's ultimately not fighting for herself, but for the scene. She sticks with her guns and doesn't let anyone mess with her when she thinks she's right." He stopped hating her guts by the time he had to do press. "I loved acting with her," he insisted. "And, although it sounds chauvinistic, Meryl is never at the mirror between shots, like a lot of actresses are. She's in the script, she's in your ear, saying why don't we try this or that? She's not going back to check her face."[73]

Putting Words in Joanna's Mouth

From her very first meeting about the film, Streep had felt that her primary job was to enrich the character of Joanna so that she wouldn't be a mere villain.

"It's not necessary that you sympathize with her," she noted. "It's not even necessary that you understand her. But she must be realistic. In the book, I hated her. I didn't understand her, and she was no one I'd ever known. I want to make it a little harder for the audience to place its allegiance."[74] She was taking material that could well be interpreted as "antifeminist" and, by enriching the experiences and depth of feeling of the woman at its center, enacting a kind of feminism. In this case, the choices that matched

Opposite: Joanna must go to court to fight for custody of her son.

Ted and his son, Billy (Justin Henry), come up with new ways to make things work after Joanna leaves.

her personal beliefs also made for better drama. "If there's a white hat–black hat situation," Streep said, "that doesn't make for an interesting courtroom scene, which I consider the climax of the film."[75]

Writer/director Robert Benton agreed that the courtroom scene, in which Joanna states her case for custody and Ted's lawyer aggressively pokes holes in that case, was crucial. Seeking an authentic female point of view, he suggested that Streep use her own words. But when the actress actually showed up on set having rewritten her dialogue, Benton was nervous. "I thought, oh my God, I'm going to lose two days' work. One, rewriting what she's done, and the other soothing her wounded feelings," he said. "Well, her scene was brilliant. I cut only two lines. What you see there is hers."[76] He added, "In fact, it was the best 'writing' in the picture."[77]

Streep's dialogue successfully articulates Joanna's position and the emotional quagmire common to many women. As Joanna, she defends the desire to find fulfillment both at work and at home ("Just because I needed some kind of creative or emotional outlet other than my child, that didn't make me unfit to be a mother"), while confidently dropping buzzwords of then-trendy psychology ("I have worked very, very hard to become a whole human being. And I don't think I should be punished for that.") But it's not what she says

that earns our sympathy so much as how Streep conveys the courage it required for Joanna to make it into that room in order to say those words, and the way she shows how her stockpiled strength is worn down by the process of cross-examination. When Ted's lawyer accuses her of having failed as a wife, she looks at him coolly and says softly, but insistently, "I was not a failure. […] I consider it less my failure than his." But the lawyer badgers her until her eyes flood with tears—which reads as an admission of guilt.

After Joanna returns to the film, Streep powerfully makes the case that this woman who abandoned her family had no choice, that she couldn't survive in that marriage sacrificed to the rat race, that the patriarchal, corporate way of life zaps everyone in it of their individual humanity. But as much as Benton made an effort to add balance to this battle of the sexes, in the end the two sides are given nothing like equal attention—far more emotional weight, and screen time, is devoted to Ted's struggles. By design, there is a winner and a loser in this fight; in the end, the woman who was driven to breakdown by life as a housewife, forced to seek fulfillment and identity outside the home, finds that she can't go home again. The very essence and structure of the film is patriarchal. That Streep manages to do anything to even the scales is a small miracle.

"Films are nice, but I don't live in this world," Streep said in 1979, on the verge of costarring in *Kramer vs. Kramer*. "Movies aren't going to be my life. I come in, do my job and don't hang around." She added, "I can put more energy into plays, I can involve my whole body, I can open my mouth and scream." Having appeared triumphantly in ten New York theater productions between 1975 and 1979, Streep was positioning herself as a stage actress who would occasionally dabble in movies, so that one medium would inform the other. As she put it, "to be in a vacuum with just Joanna Kramer would make for a boring Joanna Kramer. It's theater that sustains me."[d]

Ironically, a stage production Streep worked on simultaneously with *Kramer* would turn out to be her final theatrical effort for twenty years. Streep began workshopping *Alice in Concert*, an all-sung version of *Alice's Adventures in Wonderland*, with writer/composer Elizabeth Swados and director Joseph Papp in 1979, and in December 1980, the show opened at the Public Theater to dismal reviews. Frank Rich, writing in the *New York Times*, called Streep the "one wonder" of the production but added, "one still must wonder why she has devoted so much

energy to this show, dating back to its original workshop presentation two years ago. Maybe, like Carroll's heroine, this actress took a drink from a mysterious bottle labeled 'Drink Me' and then, quite unwittingly, lost her head."[e] Streep concentrated on her film career for the next two decades, turning down an offer from Papp to take his place as director at the Public Theater in the early 1990s in order to keep her focus on acting. Her home life was also an issue: as all-consuming as movies can be, she could bring her kids on location, but a play would have taken her away from the family dinner table every night.

She finally returned to the stage in 2001 to star in a free Central Park production of a new adaptation of *The Seagull*, directed by Mike Nichols. She had been missed. For the *New York Times*' Ben Brantley, it was "indeed nice to have this Oscar-winning actress back where she belongs,"[f] and the *Village Voice*'s Michael Feingold concurred: "In her beauty, her unforced assurance, and her frisky energy, she seems to have picked up exactly where the Streep of 20 years ago left off."[g]

Streep has starred in only one other theatrical production since her long hiatus, but it was an even greater triumph: Tony Kushner's adaptation of Bertolt Brecht's *Mother*

Courage and Her Children, which had a spectacular four-week run in 2006 while the polar-opposite *Devil Wears Prada* was in theaters. That simultaneous one-two punch did much to bring Streep's persona down to earth. As critic Hilton Als wrote of Streep's *Mother Courage* performance in *The New Yorker*, "Her grandeur is merely a façade, she seems to be telling us, and she is as committed to the job at hand as any other conscientious working actress."[h] She was so committed to the job that, for the first time, Streep allowed a camera to document her process, resulting in the documentary *Theater of War* (2008). She admitted that she did so with reluctance: "I never let anybody see process, because process is clunky. Process looks like bad acting."[i]

Meryl Streep (Alice) and Rodney Hudson in *Alice in Concert*, written by Elizabeth Swados and directed by Joseph Papp, in 1980 during the New York Shakespeare Festival.

The Movie of the Year

Like *The Deer Hunter*, *Kramer* reflected a cultural shift away from the progressive social movements of the 1960s and early 1970s, and into Reagan-era conservatism; in both films, Streep embodies the trauma that shift caused for women whose options are limited. And, Streep appears in both in the beginning and then in a later act, her absence in some way structuring the male protagonists' personal evolutions. Both films are the stories of men, told from fundamentally patriarchal perspectives, in which Streep enables us to see the pain and confusion of having the narrative of one's life proscribed by someone else.

Kramer was released in December 1979—the year the divorce rate hit an all-time peak, when right-wing conservatives were successfully drumming up panic that the long-debated Equal Rights Amendment, which was intended to abolish gender discrimination, would actually ensure "the takeaway of rights women already have."[78] In this climate, the film hit a nerve. "The characters are very much citizens of the 1970s," wrote critic Frank Rich. "Their troubles illuminate the cutting edge of an era when all the old definitions of marriage and family have been torn apart."[79]

Kramer's politics were chewed over by critics and political pundits on all sides, with Streep's performance serving as a litmus test for the audience's reactions. "At the screening I attended," wrote Michael Sragow, "she was roundly hissed."[80] "The major weakness of the film is the conception of Joanna's character," agreed Stephen Farber. "Joanna spouts a lot of feminist rhetoric about finding herself; the liberal sentiments are impeccable, but they're too vague and hackneyed to register with much force [... but] Meryl Streep brings her own emotional intensity to the part. She is one of those rare performers who can imbue the most routine moments with a hint of mystery."[81]

In April, *Kramer* swept the Oscars—Hoffman and Streep both won acting awards, and writer/director Benton took home two trophies of his own—but the plaudits didn't end debate over the film. At the awards, Team Kramer got into a confrontation with Rona Barrett, a Hollywood reporter who had reviewed *Kramer* harshly. Strolling backstage after his win, Hoffman addressed Barrett directly, taunting her with a reference to her review. Barrett responded with a challenge: "Many feminists and many women who have seen the film feel that the picture in essence was a slap to them because it says one parent has to be better than the other and that is the father."[82]

Streep jumped in. "Well, here comes a Feminist," she said. "I don't feel that at all. I think the basis of feminism has something to do with liberating men and women from proscribed roles." While she was speaking, Hoffman sat on the floor at Streep's feet, dangling his legs over the side of the press room stage. Streep joined him. As one reporter observed, "No posturing, no effect at keeping up a dignified front. Just a couple of nice people relaxing and talking to some of the most influential entertainment news people in the nation."[83]

If Streep seemed "relaxed," that in itself was a feat of acting. She was, in fact, so overwhelmed with nerves that she forgot her Oscar statuette in the backstage bathroom. "It's very nerve-wracking," she admitted later. "I threw up for three days at the Beverly Hills Hotel. Then it happened and we went home. I can't take that."[84]

By "we," Streep meant herself and Don Gummer, who she had married in September 1978, just six months after Cazale's death. Streep had been forced to vacate the apartment she and Cazale had shared after he died. Gummer, who was friends with Streep's brother, Harry William, and happened to be about to depart on an around-the-world trip, suggested she stay at his place. While Gummer was away, he and Streep became pen pals. They married two months after Gummer returned. "It just seemed right,"[85] Streep said simply in 1980.

How did she get over Cazale and move on so quickly? "I didn't get over it," she insisted. "I don't want to get over it. No matter what you do, the pain is always there in some recess of your mind, and it affects everything that happens afterwards." But, she added, "I think you can assimilate the pain and go on without making an obsession of it."[86]

A month before *Kramer* opened, Streep gave birth to her first child, Henry. She was thirty, and, unlike the woman she'd win an Oscar for playing, she had consciously put off motherhood until she felt secure in her career. "I wanted first to know I could make it as an actress," she said. "Being a mother alone without a career would not have been satisfaction enough—neither would being a star but single and childless. Basically I want it all—but in manageable portions."[87]

After several months of separation, Joanna finds Billy again in Central Park.

3

Sophie Zawistowska

Sophie's Choice (1982)
Alan J. Pakula

"It's easier to live in New York when my big face isn't being smeared all over the place. Magazine stands make me sick. I want to keep my life private, give my kid a break."[88]
—Meryl Streep, 1983

With *Kramer vs. Kramer*, Streep became the Oscar-winning star of the biggest film of the year, and this catapulted her to a new level of fame—one she wasn't prepared for. By the first week of 1980, barely more than year after the release of her first significant film, she was on the cover of *Newsweek*, her face above an auspicious headline: "A Star for the '80s."

Inside the magazine, Jack Kroll explained what made Meryl Streep the poster child of her time. "There's a sense of mystery in her acting; she doesn't simply imitate (although she's a great mimic in private). She transmits a sense of danger, a primal unease lying just below the surface of normal behavior." Streep, he went on, was also an improvement over other female actresses of her era, "less ingratiating than Jill Clayburgh, less self-satisfied than the recent Jane Fonda [...] and unlike the Great Bimbos of the 70s, the Farrah [Fawcett]s and the Suzanne [Somers]s, her beauty has nothing to do with the yearning smirks of male fantasy. Farrah smiles like a plastic nutcracker. Streep smiles like destiny."[89]

"For a while there it was either me or the Ayatollah on the covers of national magazines," Streep sighed in 1981. "It was excessive hype."[90]

As her celebrity was peaking, she took special care to concentrate on her family. It was a controversial decision. "I had Henry the day after we finished the reshoot of the last scene of *Kramer*," she said. "Then I took a year off and people said, 'You're crazy. Now that *Kramer* is going to come out, you can do anything you want—it's the wrong time.' But I think you do what you have to do to make you happy."[91]

Streep still had not committed to Hollywood stardom over the life of a New York theater actress; she was not exactly thrilled by the film roles she was being offered. "I get sent lots and lots of heroines and nice girl parts," she complained in 1979. "You know. There's some man who moves the plot, and his sidekick is a girl who has one nude scene and is vulnerable and kind of funny at times... the kind of thing you just never want to see again. I want to do something gritty, something real funny, a real smelly part."[92] Two years later, she told her agent, "I've got to do something outside of Manhattan, outside of 1981, outside of my experience. Put me on the moon; I want to be someplace else. I want to be held in the boundaries of a different time and place."[93]

She took a dual role in Karel Reisz's *The French Lieutenant's Woman* (1981), as Sarah, a nineteenth-century British woman with a bad reputation, and Anna, a twentieth-century actress playing Sarah in a movie within the movie. Streep was happy with her performance, although she fretted that she had been miscast: "Watching the film, I couldn't help wishing that I was more beautiful. There comes a point when you have to look the part, especially in movies... I really wished I was the kind of actress who could have just stood there and said it all."[94] She did exactly that in her next film, which offered a gritty, smelly part for the ages.

The Farce of "Choice"

William Styron's 1979 novel *Sophie's Choice* was both a thinly veiled memoir of the author's personal experience sharing a Brooklyn boarding house with a beautiful Polish Holocaust survivor, and a meditation on memory, guilt, and responsibility tied to the defining moral catastrophes of both the twentieth century (the Holocaust) and the American antebellum era (slavery). It's a story of a woman destroyed by a very specific, still freshly painful war; it's also a universal story about first love and its loss. The 1982 film version, written and directed by Alan J. Pakula, is austere and maybe even too tasteful in its depiction of the horrors of the Holocaust, but boldly expressionist in its treatment of how those who survived those horrors could be destroyed by their memories, even after they were theoretically "safe." A film about a single woman in an impossible situation, its very title became a kind of cultural catchphrase, shorthand for irreconcilable polarities of any and every kind.

The movie is structured as a love triangle between Stingo (the young, naïve writer based on Styron), Nathan (a charismatic but crazy New York Jewish intellectual), and Sophie (the concentration camp survivor both men love).

Meryl Streep as Sophie Zawistowska in Alan J. Pakula's *Sophie's Choice* (1982).

Opposite, top and bottom: The love triangle made up of Nathan (Kevin Kline), Sophie (Meryl Streep), and Stingo (Peter MacNicol) in the film adaptation of William Styron's novel.

Kevin Kline, Meryl Streep, and Alan J. Pakula on set in New York.

The backbone of the movie is formed by the numerous scenes in which Sophie tells versions of her own history, which, as the film unfolds, are revealed to be subjective and, in some cases, carefully fabricated to conceal the truth. As Sophie becomes closer to Stingo, the film teases the notion that her character's "choice" might be as trifling as the choice between two mates, only to reveal that she actually made her choice during the war, when she was forced to decide which of her two children was to be sent to a work camp and which was to be exterminated immediately. Wracked with guilt—she's unable to acknowledge that she did the only things she could to survive in a situation set up to destroy her—she slips into denial, fabricating fantasy versions of her history. Her "choice" during the war, of course, is a farce, and through the course of the film we come to understand that because of all she's been through, she has no real choices after the war, either. The title, finally, seems to be ironic. The film reveals the fallacy of approaching life, or history, as a set of binary, true/false, right/wrong oppositions. As Sophie admits in a moment of desperate confession, "The truth? I don't even know what is the truth after all these lies that I've told."

Fighting to Play Sophie

Alan Pakula was initially determined to select three unknowns for the key parts of Stingo,

Nathan, and Sophie. Eventually he decided that, for commercial reasons, he needed at least one star, but he wasn't sure which part to cast up.

The first option was to use a male movie star to play Nathan—Pacino, Hoffman, De Niro—and then cast a European unknown as Sophie. Pakula set his eyes on Slovak actress Magda Vásáryová. But then Polish director Andrzej Wajda contacted Pakula and suggested Streep—who had secretly obtained a copy of the script and was dying to play the role.

"Pakula saw me as a courtesy to my agent,"[95] Streep remembered. They met in his office, which was not the most welcoming environment for Streep—the walls were plastered with photos of Vásáryová. "I don't mean two pictures, I mean maybe 20 pictures, all different poses of her," Streep recalled. "But he listened to me. He not only listened, he said 'Come back next week and we'll talk again.' I came back—twice. Then he let me sit by my telephone for two and a half weeks before he called me."[96] Ultimately, she says, after another visit to Pakula's office and a promise to learn Polish, "He let another two days go by and said, 'Well, you and the studio have won.'"[97] Why did Pakula hem and haw so over casting the "Star of the '80s" in *Sophie's Choice*? "I knew it would be a beautiful performance but I was afraid that you'd see the technique, the actress acting," the writer/director said. "In the second place, in everything I'd seen her do, she'd played a strong

Upon arriving in New York, Sophie, a concentration camp survivor, meets Nathan, a charismatic but unpredicable Jewish intellectual.

Opposite: Meryl Streep on the set.

Following pages: After yet another violent fight, Nathan and Sophie's relationship is on shaky ground.

women, and I felt she was too strong for the self-doubting woman Sophie is. And in the third place, I must say I hadn't seen in her other work the kind of sensuality, the abandonment, that is also part of Sophie." When the film was finished, Pakula admitted, "I was absolutely wrong on all three counts."[98]

The Transformation

As a New Jersey girl, Meryl Streep might have been an unlikely candidate for the role of Sophie, but she had a visceral connection to the material. As an adult, she was still haunted by a photo she had seen when she was ten, of an abandoned Lebensborn transport full of children's corpses. "The piled-up bodies on the truck... I will never forget that image," she said years later, choking up. "It forms the basis of my understanding of unimaginable horror."[99]

Like *Kramer*, *Sophie* was based on a popular novel; it would also feature Streep, now a mom herself, playing a woman so guilt-ridden over her failures as a parent that she tells a man who loves her that it "would not be fair to your children to have me as a mother." But it's hard to overestimate what a giant leap forward this role would represent for Streep.

In 1981, Streep had never fully transformed herself on-screen. Previous parts had required Streep to adopt an accent, such as the Southern

belle in *Joe Tynan*, but Sophie presented a much higher level of difficulty. How would she approach becoming a Polish immigrant who had arrived in America in a state of starvation after enduring unimaginable horrors at Auschwitz? "First I'll learn Polish," Streep said six months before the shoot. "Then I'll forget me. Then I'll get to her."[100]

It took Streep a while to "get to her," to find the kernel within Sophie that the actress could personally relate to. "The problem was that Sophie was such a victim," Streep said. "She really let the tanks run over her."[101] Sophie is also incredibly sexualized, her effect on the male gaze most apparent when she is at her most vulnerable and powerless. In flashbacks to wartime, her womanliness is treated as currency, and in the present day, her trauma partially manifests itself in a sadomasochistic relationship with Nathan. While both Linda and Joanna were, like Sophie, to some extent victims of merely having been born female in the wrong place and wrong time, Sophie's almost vulgar physical abandon was nothing like anything Streep had played before. Many years later, while working on another piece about a woman in war, Tony Kushner's 2006 revival of *Mother Courage and Her Children*, Streep would explain that she had felt "despair and rage about who gets mowed under in these wars of ideology," embodied by "the scene we see over and over, on television, and everywhere:

Throughout the decade and half over which their careers overlapped, Meryl Streep was a *bête noire* of film critic Pauline Kael. Kael offered perhaps her most vicious assessment of the actress in her review of *Sophie's Choice*, in which she theorized that "by bringing an unwarranted intensity to one facet of a performance, [Streep] in effect decorporealizes herself. This could explain why her movie heroines don't seem to be full characters, and why there are no incidental joys to be had from watching her." [j] Five years later, in a conversation with an old friend, playwright Wendy Wasserstein, published in *Interview* magazine, Streep mused at length about what she saw as a disconnect between film critics and the art of acting.

"So many people who write about the movies don't understand […] the process of the creation of the actor. They don't know what it is. I've been thinking about this for a long time. I always wanted to get together a group of actors and talk about the process and write it all down and send it to all the major critics so they'd know what actors do. I don't think they do know. They judge it, yet they don't know what it is that they are looking at. Most of them—even the most sophisticated—are swept away by whether it's a character they like or dislike. They confuse the dancer with the dance. With my work, they get stuck in the auto mechanics of it—the most obvious stuff, like what's under the hood. They mention the accent or the hair—as if it's something I've laid on that doesn't have anything to do with the character. It's very ingenuous, really. They're like children who want to believe in Santa Claus. Some critics categorically refuse to believe that Santa Claus is their dad with a beard. That it really is that person, that Jack Nicholson *is* like Jack Nicholson. The news is that most of the great practitioners of the art of acting know exactly what they're doing; even in the best, most successful moments, when they let go of the awareness of what they are doing, they still, somewhere deep inside their body, *know* what they're doing. There is a craft." [k]

Women just going, 'Why?' over the bodies of their children. 'Why?!?'"[102] It stands to reason that this compassion for the price inflicted on women as collateral damage from the political conflicts of men helped her to connect to Sophie. Eventually, she said, "I saw little bits of me in her. I found she had some spirit, a little backbone. After everything that hits her, she just sort of gets up with a lot of life and vitality. I liked that."[103]

Here Streep's grab bag approach included some elements reminiscent of Method acting. She studied Polish for several months before rehearsals, and it wasn't easy for her. "Getting your mouth around those sounds is very hard," she admitted. Once she mastered the accent, she spoke with it continuously throughout the production. "There is at least a trace of accent even in her casual set-side conversation," noted journalist Charles Champlin when he visited the set, "and it seems nothing like an affectation, more like a superstitious homage to a spell that must not be broken."[104] Pakula later recalled the first time he heard Streep read lines with her Polish accent: "I thought at first, 'Oh no, this isn't going to be any good,' because I didn't believe it was coming from her. And then I realized it was the shock of hearing her become a different person."[105]

Pakula shaped the production more like a play than a traditional film set. The cast rehearsed for a full three weeks, to give the actors time to get to know each other and build trust with their director. After shooting began, Pakula was open to improvisation. "We did spontaneous things," Streep said. "We fooled around in different ways,"[106] confirmed Kevin Kline, who was cast as Nathan. "Alan encouraged us to keep exploring, improvising. If things started getting too rigid, Meryl would say, 'Let's do it messy again.'"[107]

Streep appreciated Pakula's approach. "You'd be surprised by how many people start movies on the basis of rehearsing eight days," she said while on set. "In film it's very easy to be interested only in what you're doing. But Alan was really interested in all of our ideas about all of the movie. In rehearsal we talked about structure, the arc of the characters, things like that. It's right out of the theater tradition."[108]

The transformation was physical, too. To play the postwar Sophie during the film's present-tense scenes, Streep gained a few pounds (to better convey the survivor's lust for life, and just plain lustiness), and wore prosthetic teeth. "That's not the way Meryl sounds or the way she really looks," Pakula commented. "She had false teeth, because Sophie would have lost all her teeth in the concentration camp. It was remarkable. And when she spoke Polish, she looked different." The writer/director acknowledged the profound impact of his star's performance: "I still, in middle age at that time, was Stingo, too, falling in love."[109]

Which isn't to say he was so blinded by his admiration of his actress as to defer to her entirely.

In one scene in which Stingo and Sophie get drunk together, Streep wanted to drink real alcohol. "I thought, most actors can't handle that, but she has such great technique," Pakula said. He let Streep play the scene her way. But when the dailies came back, the director thought the actress's performance was too over-the-top to use. "I don't know that she ever agreed with me," he admitted. "But I agreed with me."[110]

Such disagreements aside, Pakula noted, "There was a camaraderie on this film that was very special."[111] Streep knew Kevin Kline from the theater world, and she cannily used her camaraderie with him to draw an emotional response from Peter MacNicol, who played Stingo. After they started shooting, the younger actor approached Pakula to complain that Streep was ignoring him. "She's obsessed with Kevin Kline, and she doesn't pay much attention to me," he said. "It's destroying my morale." Pakula confronted Meryl about it, and she responded, "Alan, at this point, I'm in love with Kevin Kline and [Peter's character] means very little to me, he's a stranger. His time will come."[112]

A Master Class in Acting for the Camera

The theater-trained Streep had previously struggled to act for the camera, but *Sophie's Choice* is nothing if not a master class in the symbiotic relationship between an actress and the lens. Streep was quick to acknowledge the ways in which her performance was supported and enhanced by the decisions made by Pakula and his crew, particularly cinematographer Nestor Almendros, who she credited with giving her the isolation she needed to conjure Sophie's confession to Stingo of her experience in Auschwitz.

"Sophie was seeing through the layers of her memory into what happened then," Streep said. "Nestor conceived of shooting this memory from outside of the house. And since the camera was way far away, I thought they were far away, so I felt completely alone. And I was alone—with my memory."[113] Though the glass of the window is not visible on-screen, this technique gives Streep's face, seen in extreme close-up, a hazy quality, which helps to soften her makeup-smeared face, making it easier for the audience to absorb her direct address to the camera. It feels as though she's speaking directly to us, and yet she's also somehow out of reach—no matter how transparent her confession, there's some aspect of her experience, of her pain, that we will never be able to know.

After the New York portion of the shoot wrapped, Streep and the crew had some time off before decamping to Yugoslavia for three weeks to film Sophie's flashbacks of wartime. It turned out Streep needed all the "time off" she could get: Pakula had written all the flashbacks in English,

When Stingo begs Sophie to tell him the truth about her past, she has to reject all the lies she's told so far and recall what really happened in Poland.

Following pages: Thrown off by Nathan's behavior, Sophie begins to grow closer to Stingo.

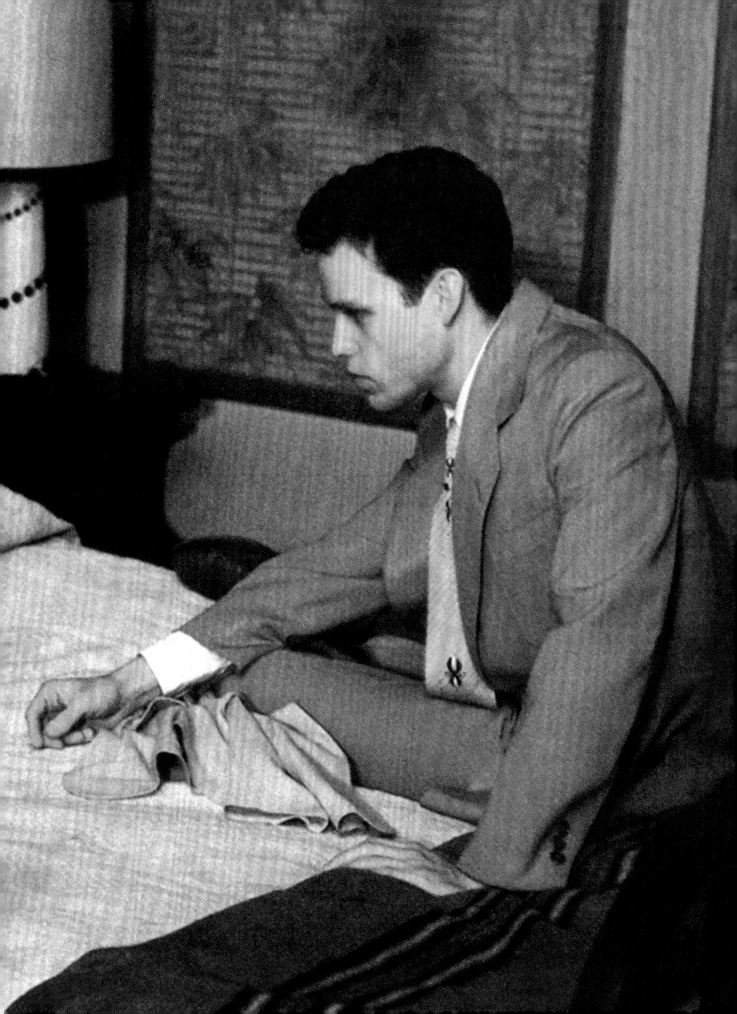

Pakula and Streep filming one of the Auschwitz scenes.

Opposite: Sophie's choice: the SS doctor (Karlheinz Hackl) forces her to choose which of her two children (Jennifer Lawn and Adrian Kalitka) will be exterminated immediately.

but shortly before heading to Europe he decided he had to film them in Polish and German. "Poor Meryl had just been sweating out the Polish accent," Pakula said later. "Now I'm going to say, 'You're going to have to learn German'?"

"With fear and trepidation," Pakula approached his star. "I said, 'Meryl, you're gonna kill me, but we have to do this, we have to separate from the American part because it's another world, and we really should feel the other languages, otherwise it's not gonna work. And I should have told you six months ago.' Streep said, 'Get me a German teacher.'"[114]

Streep's other challenge was to lose a lot of weight—all she had gained for the Brooklyn scenes, plus twenty pounds more—to play Sophie as a sickly prisoner of war, and to further help define the contrast between the different worlds Sophie inhabits. The *Los Angeles Times* reported on that aspect of the process as though it was a lark, flippantly noting that during the shoot in Yugoslavia, Streep "ate nothing at all but sustained herself completely on the local Riesling." Streep herself was quoted as saying, "It's great wine. And it costs just 40 cents a bottle. For those three weeks I was happy, drunk, and getting slimmer every day."[115] Jennifer Lawn, the child actress cast as Sophie's daughter, was not so happy with the transformation. Streep had spent a lot of time with the young actress, and they became very close; Lawn was very upset to see her pretend

mother appear so emaciated. As she had done with MacNicol in Brooklyn, Streep was using her process to illicit unpleasant but appropriate emotional responses from her costars.

Given such anecdotes showing Streep's level of savvy as a performer and as a member of the ensemble, it's a surprise to learn that when it came to the film's most pivotal and wrenching scene, in which we finally see Sophie make her "choice," Streep went in without a game plan. "I couldn't even read that scene, of the choice," Streep admitted. "I read it once, when we got the script, and then I never read it again. Because I couldn't stand it… because I was Sophie, I was in denial."[116]

Speaking German, without the false teeth she wears in the Brooklyn scenes, in the flashback to the choice Streep sounds and looks markedly different from the present-day Sophie who is remembering it. When Sophie's daughter is carried away, she screams—but no sound comes from her mouth. Her daughter's screams fill the sound track as we watch Sophie in silent agony. The pairing of sound and image communicates that this is not only the last time Sophie will see or hear her daughter, but the last moments of Sophie's life as she knew it. She has literally lost her voice. "I thought I was screaming," Streep later said. "I thought I was screaming as loud as I could. It was like being in a dream. You realize that no sound is coming out later, but you really think you're screaming."[117]

Streep's performance as Sophie is both realistic and heightened beyond realism. The overall effect calls to mind Streep's comments about what she had learned by watching Liza Minnelli: to pair "truth-telling" with "brilliance, sparkle and excitement" to "attract the audience to your character."[118] In the case of *Sophie's Choice*, pure naturalism wouldn't have been as effective; Streep needed to add that layer of gloss to make the ultimate emotional connection.

Coming Into Her Stardom

When it came time to promote *Sophie*, Streep was pregnant with her daughter Mamie, who would be born in August 1983. She sat out the Los Angeles press tour on doctor's orders, but made the rounds of the pre–Oscar awards circuit to accept accolades. Still, she guarded her privacy fiercely, and it was perceived that she was doing the bare minimum to campaign for an Oscar. As one anonymous observer quipped, "Meryl arrives late, sits with her husband, and flees after dinner. No chitchat." Perhaps Streep felt there was no need to overextend herself: *People* predicted that Jessica Lange, nominated for *Frances* (1982), was Streep's "only competition of consequence in the Best Actress race."[119]

Sophie's Choice was not particularly well reviewed, but Streep's performance earned raves. *Variety* called the film "astoundingly tedious."[120] Peter Rainer sniffed, "With the exception of Meryl Streep's performance, the whole enterprise seems embalmed."[121] Joy Gould Boyum spotted the extent to which the filmmaking framed the performance: "Pakula literally gives the film to Meryl Streep, holding his camera on her, and using closeup to an extent that only Ingmar Bergman has dared before him. She rises to it; her voice, with its perfectly convincing Polish accent; her suggestive expressions; her revealing gestures, all are endlessly absorbing."[122]

But it was Pauline Kael's withering review of what she labeled "an infuriatingly bad movie" that would haunt Streep for years. "I felt more sympathy for Meryl Streep, the actress trying to put over these ultimate-horror scenes, than I could for Sophie herself. [...] She has, as usual, put thought and effort into her work. But something about her puzzles me: after I've seen her in a movie, I can't visualize her from the neck down [...] This could explain why her movie heroines don't seem to be full characters, and why there are no incidental joys to be had from watching her. It could be that in her zeal to be an honest actress she allows nothing to escape her conception of a performance. Instead of trying to achieve freedom in front of the camera, she's predetermining what it records."[123]

"I'm incapable of not thinking about what Pauline wrote," Streep admitted in 2008. "And you know what I think? That Pauline was a poor

Jewish girl who was at Berkeley with all these rich Pasadena Wasps with long blonde hair, and the heartlessness of them got her. And then, years later, she sees me."[124]

In the end, come Oscar night, the Academy Award did indeed go to, as presenter Sylvester Stallone put it, "marvelous Meryl Streep." The substantially pregnant star, draped in a billowing cloud of gold sequins (a Sonia Rykiel creation loaned to her by Cher), took the stage and clumsily dropped her written speech. Laughing at herself, her head in her hands, she elicited a warm chuckle from the crowd. "Oh, boy!" she exclaimed, blushing. "No matter how you try to imagine what this is like, it's just so incredibly thrilling, right down to your toes." Her breathy self-consciousness was ingratiating—and it must have seemed like a sharp contrast to the ice queen who stared out from the cover of magazines, who refrained from "chitchat" at gala dinners. She thanked Styron and Pakula, the film's financiers, many members of the crew, her German and Polish coaches, and the cast—specifically, Kline and MacNicol. "I feel that I owe them this, because everything I had, I got from looking in their eyes."[125]

Backstage, speaking to the collected press, a journalist reminded Streep that in the run-up to the awards, she had said she hoped she wouldn't win, so that she could remain an underdog in Hollywood. Now that she had the statuette in hand, did she still feel that way? For a moment, Streep seemed like a different woman from the one who bristled at her own media coverage, cowering from the spotlight and fiercely defending her family's privacy. She laughed and shook her head vigorously. "No, no, no, no, no!"[126]

Nathan and Sophie's complicated relationship can survive neither his mental disorder nor her obsessions.

Karen Silkwood

Silkwood (1983)
Mike Nichols

"I felt we were a lot alike. And another thing that's the same. If I die, nobody will know what I was really like, and that's the truth." [127]
—Meryl Streep on playing Karen Silkwood

Drew Stephens (Kurt Russell)—studly, prone to completing household tasks with his shirt off—has quit his job at the Kerr-McGee plutonium processing plant in rural Oklahoma and is moving out of the house he shares with Karen Silkwood (Meryl Streep), his coworker/lover. Karen—scrawny but with a tomboy carnality, ratty brown mullet and all—has recently become obsessed with safety issues at the plant, a concern that has manifested in her devoting her free time to working with the union. This newfound obsession on the part of his formerly fun-loving girlfriend has become a drag for Drew. He's packing his car to go. She asks him to stay. "Sweetheart, it's like you're two people," complains Drew. "I'm in love with one of them. But the other one is…" Karen finishes his sentence: "Just a real pain in the ass."

In real life, Karen Silkwood, long a committed union activist, died in 1974 in a suspicious car accident on her way to a meeting with a reporter from the *New York Times*, to whom she had promised to hand photographic evidence that the Kerr-McGee plant at which she worked was consciously exporting deficient fuel rods. The incriminating material was not found in the wreckage of Silkwood's car, fueling conspiracy theories that she was silenced; her autopsy showed alcohol and Quaaludes in her system, supporting Kerr-McGee's argument that she was responsible for her own demise. In death Silkwood became, as one journalist put it, "a symbol of all the courageous common people who dare to pit themselves against the giants of industry or government without regard for personal consequences." [128]

Mike Nichols's 1983 film *Silkwood* was written, by Alice Arlen and Nora Ephron, with Streep in mind, but because of the real Silkwood's larger-than-life reputation, Streep felt she had her work cut out for her. "Karen Silkwood has come to stand for so many things to so many people that I had to start all over again in trying to play her as a person, not a symbol." [129]

At the start of the film, Karen has apparently never felt a strong sense of responsibility, to herself or those around her. But after a series of bodily contaminations in her workplace, Silkwood wakes up. Her transformation into a muckraking activist comes at the expense of her contented, if messy, personal life. For the first time playing a character based on a real person, Streep connected to the material as a story about how consciousness happens, how it can change a person, and how that type of change is incompatible with traditional female roles and male expectations.

An American Tragedy

In the first scenes of *Silkwood*, Karen swaps shifts with a coworker so that she can take a weekend trip to visit her kids, who live with their dad hours away. While she's away, there's a contamination scare, and Karen, who had joked about wishing for a disaster so she wouldn't have to work over the weekend, is blamed for it. Then she's contaminated herself, forced to undergo a painful scrubbing process and to submit daily urine tests. Transferred to another department, she learns that the company has been covering up errors in the manufacturing of nuclear fuel rods. This awareness leads to politicization—a show of extracurricular activity that doesn't sit well with her housemates, boyfriend Drew and best friend Dolly (Cher).

"She isn't isolated at the beginning of the story. There aren't nine million closeups," Streep noted, demonstrating her increasingly sophisticated understanding of screen performance. "The camera stays back, at a distance. You feel she's part of the life of everybody in her house and in the plant. Then, after a while, the camera moves in on her." [130] As her activism consumes her, Karen is increasingly depicted in contrast against a community of coworkers who are hostile toward the squeaky wheel, convinced that her efforts with the union will endanger their livelihoods—a bigger concern than the job itself endangering their lives. No one, Karen included, can afford to lose their job.

That Karen and friends are resigned to a life of minimal options and no recourse in bad situations is explicated in two key scenes. First, when Karen, Drew, and Dolly are driving back from a disappointing visit with Karen's kids,

For the first time in her career, Meryl Streep plays a real-life woman in Mike Nichols's *Silkwood* (1983).

Karen (Meryl Streep), Drew (Kurt Russell), and Dolly (Cher) share a house, and all three work in a plutonium processing plant.

Opposite: Karen uses her weekend off to go visit her two children, who she does not have custody of.

the two women pass a joint back and forth as Karen explains why her custody rights are limited under the dissolution of her common law marriage. Dolly, a lesbian, snorts: "Goddamn government fucks you coming and going."

Later, back at the plant, Karen complains to Drew about the accusations that she had something to do with the contamination. "Quit," he says sarcastically, adding with a snicker, "Quit and live on your savings." The plant's union president chimes in with a more serious response to Karen's complaint. "The company's gotta blame someone. Otherwise it's their fault." During this exchange, Karen catches one of the other male workers on the floor staring at her. She rips open her jumpsuit and exposes her bare breast, tells him to get lost. Drew laughs, and the union chief cracks, "Hey, Karen, you ever think about going into politics?" At this point in their lives, the notion that Karen Silkwood could be a leader is as absurd as the idea that she might have savings to live on.

Her transformation is gradual: scene by scene, Karen becomes more aware of the dangers inherent in her work, and angrier at the complacency of everyone around her. The night after a contamination, when Karen and Drew are alone, she asks Drew about the risks of radiation. "You just waking up to this?" he asks incredulously. "What do you think we're working with over there, puffed wheat?" He adds,

"If you're really worried about it, stop smoking." She raises her cigarette to her mouth and puffs in response. She's used to allowing life's frustrations to roll off her back, easily distracted by momentary simple pleasures. But this time, the anxiety won't go away.

As her activism eats away at her relationships, Karen becomes convinced that she's being poisoned as part of a cover-up. The film ends with her driving down a highway to meet the reporter from the *New York Times*. She squints at the reflection in her rearview mirror as the bright headlights of a car behind her get closer. The implication is that a car may have run her off the road, although Nichols also tells the viewer, via closing titles, that Silkwood had been driving intoxicated.

Without precisely fingering who or what was responsible, the film gives the impression that Karen Silkwood didn't have to die. That was certainly Streep's impression. "At the end of this whole experience of making this movie," she said, "I thought about those minutes before Karen's car went off the road, and I missed her. What a waste of life."[131]

"No one had any interest in seeing the movie made until Meryl Streep came along."

Silkwood started out as the passion project of Carlos Anderson, Larry Cano, and Buzz Hirsch,

Opposite: Karen lives with Drew, but her union activism weakens their relationship.

Difficulties arise with her coworker Gilda (E. Katherine Kerr), who also distances herself from Karen.

three novice producers who in the mid-1970s entered into an agreement with *Ms.* magazine, which owned Silkwood's life rights but had not, according to the *Los Angeles Times*, been able to "solve the screenplay problem."[132] Around 1975, the team was talking to Jane Fonda about producing and starring in the film, but those conversations fell apart, and Fonda herself moved on to *The China Syndrome* (1979).

Kerr-McGee tried to use the courts to stop the film from going forward; the case went to the Supreme Court, which decided in 1977 that filmmakers were protected by the First Amendment. It took four years after the victory for a financier to sign on. That changed in mid-1981, when Meryl Streep publically aligned herself with the project. According to Hirsch, "No one had any interest in seeing the movie made until Meryl Streep came along."[133]

Streep felt a personal connection to Silkwood, calling the character "closer to what I'm really like than, say, *The French Lieutenant's Woman.* I'm from a small town like she was, and I, too, went to an American high school and worked for a living. Like her, I operate on my gut feelings, my emotions, not always analyzing from a distance."[134]

Production began in Dallas, Texas, on September 7, 1982—just two and a half weeks after Streep had returned from the Yugoslavia location shoot of *Sophie's Choice*. "I was afraid about that, but actually, in an odd way, it served

the script," Streep noted. "Mike spoke of the film as being about people being asleep in their lives and waking up: 'How did I get here?' And that's exactly how I felt. One day I was in Yugoslavia and the next I found myself in a plant with a light flashing and a siren going, 'Woop woop woop.' Thinking, how did this happen?"[135]

When Streep arrived in Texas, she sequestered herself in her hotel room for a Silkwood crash course, reading all of the research, including interviews and court transcripts, that Hirsch and Cano had compiled over the years. She also spent time with Silkwood's father, and with the real Drew Stephens, the basis for the boyfriend played by Kurt Russell. "I very quickly found I didn't know whom to believe," Streep recalled. "Everybody who had known Karen had a different image of her. There were a few things people agreed on, but there were so many differences. It was as if I was hearing about several different women."[136]

Ironically, Streep was finding it more difficult to play a person who had lived than a completely fictional character. The few tangible clues Silkwood left behind were not necessarily trustworthy. Streep was haunted by a widely circulated image of the woman she was playing, taken from Silkwood's workplace ID. "She's already a ghost in that portrait," Streep thought. "She's there, and she's not there."[137] At one point, the actress listened to a tape of Silkwood's voice,

Mike Nichols has been Meryl Streep's most frequent collaborator, directing her in three feature films (*Silkwood* [1983], *Heartburn* [1986], and *Postcards from the Edge* [1990]), a play (*The Seagull* [2001]), and a TV miniseries (*Angels in America* [2003]) in the thirty years since their first job together. It's a working relationship that has survived through hits and misses and ups and downs both professional and personal.

Nichols has frequently praised Streep's ability to transform, noting that "In every role she becomes a totally new human being" [l] —no small feat, given that in each of their films, Streep has played a character based on a real woman. He's been even more effusive about the effect she has on other actors. "As she becomes the person she is portraying, the other performers begin to react to her as if she were that person," Nichols said in 1987. "Whoever is playing the lover falls in love with her, whoever is playing the villain is frightened of her, whoever is playing her friend becomes her friend, and so on. She changes the chemistry of all the relationships." [m] In 2004, Nichols claimed, "It immediately increases one's talent 1,000 percent simply to look at her in a scene." [n]

Those comments from Nichols bookended a period, between 1990 and 2001, during which he and Streep did not work together, as their relationship weathered a high-profile falling-out. In 1991, Streep fired her longtime agent Sam Cohn and left his agency after Nichols chose not to cast her in a film adaptation of *The Remains of the Day*—which Nichols did not end up directing. "I left because of something Mike did that I felt Sam should have protected me from," Streep acknowledged in 1994. "Mike knows what he did, but unfortunately Sam wore the scar." By then, she said, she and Nichols had mended fences: "Mike is someone I share an enormous amount of history with." [o]

At that point, she did not know the half of it: in 2010, Streep would participate in a documentary series called *Faces of America*, in which genealogist Henry Louis Gates Jr. would prove that Streep and Nichols were distant cousins. When Gates told Streep the news on camera, she exploded in laughter: "This is ridiculous!" [p]

Opposite: Meryl Streep and Al Pacino in *Angels in America* (2003), a miniseries directed by Mike Nichols.

Karen discovers that Kerr-McGee is knowingly sending out defective fuel rods and retouching photographic negatives.

made from a phone call with a union lawyer. "Her voice was quite a lot lower than mine, and she spoke r-e-a-l slow." She listened to it again and again, but ultimately decided to forget it. "Maybe the phone call was in the middle of the night and she was tired; maybe it was her recorder. As it was, it was wrong dramatically for the movie." The experience made Streep realize the goal behind her performance: "I wasn't just trying to replicate her. We were trying to imagine, or invent, emotional reasons for her, working backward to see if we could discover why she did all that she did."[138]

A Moral Imperative

When Streep's Silkwood first tells a pair of union lawyers that she's seen her coworker alter photographs of fuel rods to omit imperfections, the lawyer tells her, "If you're right, they could kill off two million people. There's a moral imperative involved here." Streep's face tells us that this is a moment of reckoning for Karen: for maybe the first time in her life, she's considering that one human being has a responsibility to the others they share the planet with.

Streep could relate. *Silkwood* reflects the actress's own evolving sense of political and social responsibility. At Vassar, she had sniffed at campus activism, seeing through what she described as gendered "bullshit."[139] But by the mid-1980s, Streep felt moved to action. In June 1982, she had

joined a high-profile protest in Central Park against nuclear proliferation, and later that summer, she helped to organize a star-studded benefit concert for the cause. Protective of her image, she knew the American press would "invariably make some crack about Jane Fonda"[140] if she outed herself as a politicized actress. She joked that when she was nominated for the Oscar for *Sophie's Choice*, her father made her promise to keep her speech "short, sparkling, and nonpolitical" and not mention the bomb. Still, now that she was a mother, she felt a new responsibility. "I keep thinking all the time that, in the year 2000, [my son] will be only twenty-one," she said. "I've found that as my responsibilities multiply, so does my own stake in the future of the world."[141]

Streep was careful to make sure *Silkwood* was not interpreted as a vehicle for own activism, the way *The China Syndrome* (1979) had apparently been for Fonda. "No matter what I think in my real life, in order to effectively play a part or make my imagination go, I have to be presented with a certain challenge and a character with problems. What I liked about Karen was that she wasn't Joan of Arc at all. She was unsavory in some ways and yet she did some very good things."[142]

Acting in Regular Body Type

Silkwood was Mike Nichols's first film in eight years. After quickly rising to the top ranks of his

This page and opposite: Karen's fight is incompatible with her relationships with her partner, Drew (opposite), and her friend Dolly (right). It causes tension between them.

profession in the 1960s, Nichols's movie career had been stalled by two bombs, *The Day of the Dolphin* (1973) and *The Fortune* (1975). The experience of making *Silkwood*, and of working with Streep, reenergized Nichols for filmmaking. "Directing Streep is so much like falling in love that it has the characteristics of a time which you remember as magical but which is shrouded in mystery," he said.[143]

Though they would become close friends, for Streep and Cher, it was not love at first sight. "We had to get used to each other,"[144] Streep acknowledged. The performers eventually found common ground, and each had praise for the other's instinctual way of working. Streep called Cher "a completely natural actress," noting that her costar "just felt things—with the camera going."[145] The pair's common ability to "act naturally" was crucial to Nichols's conception of the movie. As Streep explained, "A lot of so-called real life in the movies is boldface. The actors are underlining the 'reality.' What we were trying to do here was just give the regular body type."[146]

Part of the wonder of Streep's performance as Silkwood is that it all seems to be happening internally; she never allows exaggerated "tells" to flash across her face, rarely giving the audience extra information that the character wouldn't want to telegraph to the other people in the scene. Her Silkwood is thus intriguingly opaque—befitting a woman that Streep had felt was

unknowable. Likewise, Streep's performance was an enigma to her coworkers. As Nichols put it, "Nobody understands what she does and how she does it."[147]

One thing we do know is that, just as false teeth and Polish lessons were integral to Streep's performance as Sophie, external stimuli helped the actress get in the headspace of Silkwood. Streep focused on "concentrating on her experiences instead of whatever was going on in her mind. For example, Drew told me she smoked a lot. So do I, in the movie. I decided that for Karen, smoking was real important. There are times in the movie when she feels all alone and smoking is instant gratification."[148] This decision constituted a major sacrifice of actress to character. "I only like a cigarette occasionally," Streep admitted. "Having to do all that chain-smoking in the film wasn't at all pleasant."[149]

Nor was the harrowing depiction of Karen's post-contamination shower scrub pure movie magic: minus the radiation poisoning, Streep experienced what Silkwood experienced. "The scrubbing was not special effects," Streep insisted. "We had to do it more or less from scratch."[150]

"The Biggest Bitch God Ever Made"

Silkwood was released December 14, 1983—about two months after the Equal Rights Amendment was reintroduced to Congress for the final time and defeated; less than a year before Reagan would win reelection in a landslide victory over the Democrat Walter Mondale, who opposed nuclear weapons and chose a woman, Geraldine Ferraro, as his running mate. Nichols's film, centered around a woman who chose professional activism at the expense of her domestic relationships, was not exactly of a piece with the national zeitgeist. It was, however, one of several films released that year, as Jay Carr put it in an article titled "Women Are Getting a Fairer Shake," that "not only incorporate feminist perspective in almost matter-of-fact ways, but are dominated by them." *Silkwood*, he wrote, was remarkable for its depiction of "men and women […] working side by side with neither thinking anything of it. Here, if anywhere, is the real women's lib in a situation where men and women are colleagues, equals. The breakthroughs in *Silkwood* include a bit of sexual role reversal, too."[151]

That's an understatement, particularly when you compare Karen to previous Streep parts. Linda, Joanna, and Sophie were, to one extent or another, victims. Silkwood is tough, so self-sufficient that her brawny boyfriend is essentially feminized, so determined to take control over her own life and use it to speak truth to power that she can only be stopped in death. That she ultimately fails reflects how challenging such a thing would be for a real woman with few resources, but Carr was right to note that *Silkwood*'s true victory is its nonchalance regarding what would have seemed like a utopian vision of gender roles just a few years earlier.

Nora Ephron, who would later direct Streep in *Julie & Julia*, cowrote a screenplay that's full of startling examinations of gender politics woven seamlessly into the story. She used her journalism background to interview Silkwood's friends and family, culling real character details on which to base the drama. "Having Meryl Streep involved with the project from the beginning was also very helpful," Ephron said, "because we knew that she would be able to play a complicated young woman and so we were going to be free to write one."[152]

While a feminist perspective runs through the film in subtle ways, one key scene delineates how Karen sees herself as a woman and how others see her. It occurs right after Karen is contaminated and scrubbed for the first time—rendered completely physically vulnerable. Back at home, she showers while Drew waits for her in bed. She enters the bedroom fussing with her hair and nails, almost talking to herself. Shirtless, his pants unbuttoned, Drew looks at her longingly and says, "I sure wish I could take care of you," and Streep, as Karen, emits a little laugh. Drew is being sincere, but in a way, this comment is as much of a pipe dream as his earlier joke about Karen's nonexistent savings. On the one hand, he's longing for financial stability in a world in which everyone works virtually every waking moment just to get by.

He's also, though, expressing a desire to live with Karen according to a simpler, more traditional gender code, one that can't apply in their community because of economics and that wouldn't apply to a self-sufficient woman like Karen in any case.

Karen doesn't respond directly. She drifts into another room as she explains that she took science classes in high school, instead of home economics, to her mom's chagrin. "I said, 'Mama, there ain't no boys in home ec. The boys are in the science class.'" Drew rises from bed and finds Karen sitting in the adjacent kitchen. He kisses her gently, making sure not to bother the skin rubbed raw by the scrubbing. "You can be the biggest bitch God ever made," he says, "and then you turn around on me and you're like this, and I want to die." As much as he might long for a different life, at this point, he accepts all that she is, headstrong bitch and vulnerable, loving partner alike.

But her new sense of purpose messes up the equilibrium of their lives; consciousness is incompatible with her domestic situation, leading to explosive friction between Karen and both Drew and Dolly. In the film's penultimate scene, Drew and Karen are reunited after their separation, and he tries to pillow-talk her into agreeing to move out to the desert and have a kid with him. She frets that they can't procreate: "They wouldn't come out right." For the third time, we're seeing Streep play a woman who is plagued by the certainty that she is not mom material, but this is different from Joanna, who was crippled by her lack of identity, or Sophie, who could not get over the guilt of not being able to protect her children. Karen knows that what's wrong with her is not inherent; it's a side effect of her job. She is the everywoman whose work makes motherhood impossible, blown up to mythic proportions.

"Everything Political Is Personal"

Silkwood, wrote Stephen Schiff in *Vanity Fair*, "is one of the best American films in years." The film's star, he wrote, "is stiff, chilly—Streepish. And yet… even when Streep's being moon-driven and actressy, Nichols knows how to direct her. Instead of propping her up in the center of the frame and letting the camera adore her suffering, Nichols sets her to the side, where she can bounce off the other actors; one sees her listening and soaking things up, one sees how fast she is, and how funny."[153]

That rave aside, with *Silkwood* Streep again earned better reviews that the movie. "Thanks to Meryl Streep's brilliant characterization of Silkwood," wrote *Newsweek*'s Jack Kroll, "we feel [her] awakening in our own, nonradioactive bones."[154] Calling Karen Streep's "most full-bodied performance," James Wolcott thought she wasn't "very convincing as a down-home tease," but added that "her dedication and nimble,

Throughout the film, Karen Silkwood gradually realizes the dangers of plutonium processing.

Following pages: Karen with Morgan (Fred Ward) and Quincy Bissell (Henderson Forsythe).

Passing through security at the plant's entrance, Karen turns out to be contaminated again. She begins to suspect someone is trying to poison her.

Opposite: Karen gets a lecture from Hurley (Bruce McGill), her line manager, who implies that she would do anything to hurt the company, even put plutonium in her own house.

undisguised skill prove to be welcome." Like Schiff, Wolcott used the "a-word": "Actressy as Streep is, she's reaching out to us, trying to establish contact."[155]

Pauline Kael was less impressed; the critic continued what now seemed like a one-woman operation to knock Queen Streep from her pedestal. "Meryl Streep gives a very fine performance as Karen Silkwood," Kael allowed, "considering that she's the wrong kind of actress for the role." Streep, Kael insisted, was "miscasting herself": "Part of being a good movie actress is in knowing what you come across as […] but in her starring performances she has been giving us artificial creations. She doesn't seem to know how to draw on herself, she hasn't yet released an innate personality on the screen."[156]

This time, Kael was hardly the film's harshest critic. Reactions were mixed amongst the real people who *Silkwood* sought to portray. While the real Drew Stephens was pleased (he called the film "magic […] it makes a human being out of Karen instead of a myth"[157]), Silkwood's father, Bill, told reporters that he felt the movie dumbed his daughter down. "The movie made her look not very bright and a hick Tobacco Road type," he said. "Karen was brilliant. She was an A student. I'll tell you what happened. The lawyers were scared of that damn movie, and Mike Nichols didn't stick to his guns."[158]

Streep repeatedly insisted that the film was as true as it could have been, and that the facts alone were enough to spook her. "During the filming I became worried that something might happen to me too. I wrote a little note to my husband saying, 'Hi, darling. If I die you'll know who did it.' Afterwards I realized that was absurd. We were not presenting anything in the film which was not a matter of public record. We did not need to embellish the story."[159]

Streep, Cher, Arlen, Ephron, and Nichols were all nominated for Oscars; none of them won. *Silkwood* had been a slow-burn success, grossing $35.6 million, but it took seven weeks to reach the top of the box office chart. While it was perhaps the most direct reflection of real American life that Streep had ever starred in, *Silkwood* wasn't beloved by the movie industry. The film's dry, socially conscious treatment of the people versus the powerful was not exactly in lockstep with the mood of mid-1980s Hollywood; the Academy ceremony on April 9, 1984 was dominated by *Terms of Endearment* (1983).

"Earnestness, it's like the worst thing you can be," Streep would say years later at a panel discussion with Ephron and Nichols touching on *Silkwood*. "But I happen to think that everything political is personal. Everything is very, very personal."[160]

5 Karen Blixen

Out of Africa (1985)
Sydney Pollack

"Every woman interested in the rights of women—herself, her mother, her daughter, etc.—is a feminist. But I'm not active in the women's movement. Sure I'd like to be, but I'm an actress professionally, and in my private life two kids keep me very busy, every day."[161]
—Meryl Streep, 1985

Streep fought hard for the lead role in *Out of Africa*, Sydney Pollack's epic historical romance based on the life, loves, and writings of Karen Blixen (who published under the name Isak Dinesen). Streep might have been widely considered the greatest actress of her generation, but that mattered little to a director who thought she wasn't sexy enough for the part. Bloated, square, and hopelessly nostalgic for colonial privilege, *Out of Africa* became a cultural phenomenon, succeeding at the box office and the Oscars, where it won best picture. It marked the end of the first phase of Streep's career and was the completion of her transition from New York theater actress underdog to Hollywood superstar. By the end of 1985, *Boxoffice* magazine would crown Streep the biggest female box office draw alive.

Out of Africa itself is a testament to Hollywood's confused approach to gender politics in the mid-1980s. A feminist film, according to its male director, it presented its protagonist as hopelessly obsessed with marriage—giving the impression that she became a strong, independent woman only because the men in her life were so reluctant to play a traditional lord and keeper to her as a wife. The actress would struggle to find the truth in the character of Karen Blixen, and would ultimately downplay her achievement, tacitly admitting she wasn't thrilled with the film.

By now, Streep's claims that she wasn't an "active" feminist were part of her persona, serving as misdirection from the subversive feminism she enacted in the way she chose and shaped her characters behind the scenes. But despite initially sensing a problem with *Africa*'s script, Streep was unable to pull the magic trick she had managed on previous films; she was unable to save a hopelessly patriarchal vision from itself. Just as Streep herself strained to claim feminist ties while assuring that her family values were dominant, *Africa* was weakened by its desire to have it both ways.

The Road to Africa

Hollywood had been trying to figure out how to film Karen Blixen's memoirs for almost fifty years by the time screenwriter Kurt Luedtke—drawing on *Silence Will Speak*, a biography by Errol Trzebinski of British hunter Denys Finch Hatton detailing his affair with Blixen, as well as a new Dinesen bio by Judith Thurman—transformed *Out of Africa* into a love story, writing with Streep in mind. "If someone had said, 'We talked to God and there is no possible way Meryl Streep will do this role,'" said Luedtke, "I might have said the hell with it."[162]

Director Sydney Pollack thought Streep was too glacial; he wasn't initially convinced she could "ooze sex."[163] Jane Seymour was rumored to be the favorite for the role in early 1984, and she actually filmed test scenes with Robert Redford, a frequent Pollack collaborator who had been cast as love interest Denys. Finally, Streep finagled a meeting with Pollack and made sure to dress the part. "I went, pathetically, in a very low-cut blouse with a push-up bra," she would admit later. "I'm very ashamed to say it, but I did. And it worked. That's the really sad part."[164]

Pollack's memory of the meeting is that Streep put herself on display in another way: "She was so direct, so honest, so without bullshit. There was no shielding between her and me. I thought, 'If this comes out of the screen—Wow!'"[165] Still, one senses that his attraction to her remained intellectual rather than physical, as this almost backhanded compliment betrays: "One could believe that she was an intellectual, a writer. I could not have made this character believable with someone else who was a more typical movie star."[166]

"How are you supposed to know when to do what they want you to do, and when not to?"

Out of Africa is structured as aged Karen Blixen's deathbed reverie, beginning with her distorted view of the Danish high society she fled for Africa. The snowbound shooting party at which she suggests that Bror Blixen (Klaus Maria Brandauer), the brother of her unfaithful lover, marry her so that she can use his title and he can use her fortune to start a new life in Africa, has the

Sydney Pollack chose Meryl Streep for the lead role in *Out of Africa* (1985).

Opposite: In order to get away from Danish polite society, Karen Blixen (Meryl Streep) suggests to her lover's brother, Bror Blixen (Klaus Maria Brandauer), that they make a new life in Africa.

As soon as Karen arrives on the African continent, she and Bror get married.

hyperreality of a Brueghel winter landscape. Its fantastic painterly quality befits the spirit of the proposal: jumping through what she sees as an escape hatch from a stifling life, Karen is following a fantasy. "Bror, listen to me," she pleads. "I've got no life at all. They won't teach me anything useful. […] I mean, at least we're friends. We might be all right. And if we weren't, at least we'd have *been* somewhere."

Rushed to the altar minutes after arriving in Africa, Karen finds herself a wallflower at her own marriage reception. Later that night, Bror reveals he used Karen's money to buy a coffee plantation instead of a dairy farm. Confronting Bror, she makes no effort to preserve anything between them: "Next time you change your mind, you do it with *your* money." Streep says the first half of this line looking down, and then tilts her face up toward Brandauer. Through the whole maneuver, she keeps her face very tight, as though Karen believes she's in control. Bror's response—he grabs that tilted face roughly, kisses her, and warns her to "Be careful"—shows how little power, or recourse, Karen actually has.

Bror goes off on a long hunt, and then, once World War I begins, joins the British on the African front. Karen is left alone to run the coffee farm. She becomes self-sufficient almost in spite of herself, and slowly relaxes her European affectations and rigid worldview. The transformation doesn't go unnoticed. Felicity (Suzanna

Hamilton), a young white woman living with her family nearby, comes to visit for tea and declares to Karen, "Someday, I'd like to run my own show, the way you do." Karen, surprised, responds: "Is that what I do?" Felicity confirms that she sees Karen as someone who doesn't need anyone, and then admits, "I don't know much about men. I want them to like me but, er, I want to be let alone, too. I'm supposed to want to be taken, aren't I? But how are you supposed to know when to do what they want you to do, and when… not to?"

Karen soon takes the kind of decisive control that Felicity suggested she was capable of. Sick of staying home alone, she leads a massive migration of animals and servants to the front where Bror has requested supplies. After a long, dangerous journey, Karen rides into the camp, dirty, disheveled—badass. She has been changed, and liberated, by adventure.

But she is continually hurt by her trust in her husband, not more so than when she contracts syphilis from him and is forced to return to Denmark for a few months for treatment. They are reconciled when she returns to Africa, but there is not much left to their relationship; the illness has rendered Karen infertile, and she throws her energy into starting a school for natives on her land. "The school, the farm… that's what I am now," she says sadly. She has become brittle, work-obsessed, almost suspicious of

Opposite: With Bror on
the front, Karen soon takes
over the plantation and gains
her independence and
freedom.

Karen says a final farewell
to her lover, Denys
(Robert Redford).

Following pages: Gathering
to celebrate New Year's 1919,
Karen and Denys find
themselves alone together.

pleasure—side effects of the anger and grief over having been, in her mind, defeminized by her husband's excessive masculinity.

The Karen-Denys romance starts in earnest one hour and twenty minutes into a two-hour-and-forty-minute movie, when Denys invites Karen to go on safari with him. As Bror moves out of Karen's life and Denys moves in, the hardness in Streep's face relaxes. Her key facial expression as Karen in love is a slight parting of the lips, the gape of mild wonderment. At one point, nearing the peak of their long courtship, Denys takes the scarf off his own neck and uses it to dab Karen's parted lips, as if to sop up beads of anticipatory drool. The part of her that died through the trials of her marriage is, under Denys's gaze, coming back to life.

Through the dramatization of the Karen-Denys romance, the conflict articulated by Felicity becomes the key question of the film. Karen is forced to reconcile seemingly warring aspects of herself: the part that fights for independence to do meaningful work and take care of herself, and the part that wants to be loved by a man, which traditionally means allowing him a measure of control. Denys doesn't want Karen to be traditionally subservient—he loves her because of her feistiness and desire to be free—but he repeatedly refuses to give her the security of traditional commitment. That refusal is, in a sense, patronizing. He *is* forcing her to be

subservient to his will if she wants him to love her. Finally, after a fight and a separation, Karen packs up to go back to Denmark, and Denys gives a bit: he begs her to let him fly her part of the way in his plane. The implication is that they will be together, for a few more nights, at least. She agrees—and then Denys never arrives. Instead, Bror comes to Karen to tell her Denys has died in a plane crash.

When Karen receives the news, Pollack frames her in a medium shot, as Streep looks up at the camera, her lidded eyes cool. Shock spreads over her face and, instead of activating emotion within it, embalms it. When Karen speaks at Denys's funeral, Pollack finally moves in on his actress's face. She is at her true bottom—her saddest, her most humbled—when she plaintively asks God to take back the soul of the man she loved: "He was not ours." She looks down, away from the camera. "He was not mine." The scene is moving because its near-miss quality—when Pollack's camera finally gets close to Streep, she plays it as though she can't bear to be seen—perfectly encapsulates the push-pull of the Karen-Denys relationship. She had been on the verge of having him, and then he was gone. Only in Denys's death can Karen get on his wavelength about separating love from ownership. Ultimately, she seems to blame herself for not bending to his will and taking whatever she could get from him when she could.

In Africa

Pollack began as an actor, trained in the version of the Method taught by Sanford Meisner at the Neighborhood Playhouse in New York. "Of all the acting teachers," Pollack felt, "Sandy was the least mystical and jargony."[167] Pollack said he "extrapolated" Meisner's teachings into directing. "My acting experience allows me to understand what actors are going through."[168]

What the actors went through on *Africa*'s Kenyan set wasn't much fun. "There was definitely not a party atmosphere on this film," said Judith Thurman, who was on set as a consulting producer. "It was very austere, very hard work."[169]

Streep worked all but two days of the 101-day shoot. She required makeup to age between late twenties and early forties, sometimes jumping back and forth between years in a single day. Torrential rain forced delays and reshoots; where the real Karen spent months waiting out droughts, on-screen she trudged out in the midst of a storm to meet her wayward husband. And Streep brought her family to Africa, which meant she spent her "off time" being a mom.

For Streep, the roughest day on set came in shooting a scene in which Karen was meant to whip an angry lion. According to Streep, Pollack was not getting the performance out of the animal he wanted, so the director, thinking his actress couldn't hear him, whispered to the trainer to take the lion off his leash. Pollack refuted that story. "I love Meryl Streep so much, I would never ever contradict anything that she said," he cautioned. "But I would have to ask any sane person whether they believe I would actually untie a lion and let it loose on my actress! I think that's a little bit of creative memory going on."[170] Perhaps, but on the other hand, we've seen that Streep used both external stimuli (*Silkwood*'s cigarettes) and strategic psychological manipulation ("ignoring" Peter MacNicol on *Sophie*) to help authenticate a character's internal life. Whether Pollack let the lion off the leash or not, Streep's performance likely was strengthened by her fear of what could happen if he did.

Director and actress also clashed over what Blixen should sound like. Streep had been given tape recordings of Dinesen reading some of the texts on which the film was based, which she studied to find Karen's voice. But as with *Silkwood*, here a direct copy of reality wasn't going to work. "When I did it for Sydney, he said, 'Oh, no!' It was too much. She was a very old-fashioned, very aristocratic woman who had an old-fashioned manner of speaking like… people used to talk in 1930s movies. Sydney thought that audiences would cringe if I talked like that. So I pulled back a bit."[171] Years later, she admitted that her ultimate source of inspiration for Karen's accent had come from

an unlikely source: "I called up Jeremy Irons, coz I knew he had a Danish nanny and he made her read poetry into a tape, which I listened to on the way to Africa."[172]

Redford had his own problems on set. He and Streep "probably got along too well," the actor admitted. "It caused ripples. We liked to talk. We'd be off camera, between takes, taking it easy. We had a sense of humor in common. But Sydney didn't like that. He would break it up. It bothered him that I was connecting with her in some way that didn't fit his picture of me, or of us as a team. That wasn't easy to deal with, because I felt I was in a vise and I became resentful."[173] Ultimately, Redford believed that Pollack pushed him to essentially play himself rather than let him act, so as to better showcase the largesse of Streep's performance. The actress, he felt, was "encouraged to fly," whereas Redford "felt I was a symbol, not a character."[174]

Whose Africa?

Compounding a shoot that didn't need more drama, there was push back from the locals. The *Kenya Times*, a newspaper owned by the government, bashed Dinesen as a "downright racist."[175] One journalist who visited the set reported that contemporary Kenyans were "embarrassed" by the book. A controversy bubbled up when black extras discovered they were being paid less than white extras, due to what a publicist described as "a simple matter of supply and demand."[176]

Both Pollack and Redford declared that the last thing they wanted was for the production itself to function as a colonialist endeavor. Redford acknowledged that he "saw that risk of 'America abroad' films. Foreign culture has been historically difficult for American filmmakers. There's often that 'John Wayne abroad' shallowness, which is the problem of one culture misinterpreting the subtleties of another. I thought the redeeming factor might be a damn good love story, which Sydney was so good at."[177]

But when Pollack spoke about *Out of Africa*'s themes, he suggested contradictions readily apparent in the finished film, a confused tug-of-war between a desire to be progressive and a patriarchal point of view so deeply ingrained that he couldn't even see his slant. He would talk about wanting to present Africa "through her [Karen's] eyes, as a paradise lost"[178]—paying lip service to the female perspective but devaluing that perspective by suggesting that "her eyes" were clouded by romanticism. He championed Blixen's story as "feminist and unusual," and then in the next breath added, "I also saw the pictures unfolding in my mind of a landscape no one knew."[179] That he was motivated to use the apparatus of a major Hollywood movie to bottle and sell "a landscape no one knew" confirms that

When Denys invites her to go on safari, Karen is forced to confront lions.

Pollack was coming to the material, consciously or not, from a colonialist perspective.

Out of Africa's sexual politics are complicated by Pollack's approach to sex itself. Both Pakula and Nichols talked of falling a little bit in love with Streep while directing her, and you can see that feeling in the way they film her. But Pollack's camera is usually kept at a respectful distance from his star. This may be in part a mirror of the character's detachment, but one gets the sense that it owes just as much to Pollack's lack of feel for Streep's sexuality, his inability to romanticize her face.

Redford thought the film was hampered by what he saw as the director's prudishness; for instance, Pollack doesn't show Denys and Karen's consummation, but he does show this wildly independent woman nagging her lover the next day to label their relationship. "Sydney, I always felt, was afraid to express sex in an open, liberal way,"[180] Redford said. Asked about the depiction of Denys and Karen's sexual relationship, Pollack became defensive. "We do imply that they have a healthy and active sexual life. I don't do explicit love scenes, and I don't think Meryl and Bob would have wanted it either." It would've been absurd, he felt, to show the man getting "all hot and bothered while she tells stories."[181]

Pollack's claim that he didn't need to show Denys and Karen's sexual relationship contrasts with what he described as a show-don't-tell philosophy regarding the film's gender politics. "I dramatized her feminism instead of giving her speeches," Pollack said. "She runs the farm. She fights off a lion. She matches each man. What I wanted to capture, without knocking the audience over the head with it, was the difference in Blixen and Finch Hatton's outlook on the degree of freedom and obligation in a relationship. She thought that if you said 'I love you,' there was a lot of obligation entailed. He thought that the reason you were with someone you loved was that you chose to be there."[182]

Their warring perspectives are quite problematically dramatized via arguments. At one point, Denys asks Karen how the wedding she's been pushing for would change their relationship. "I would have someone of my own," she says. "No," he insists. "You wouldn't." Denys echoes the problem at the heart of *Kramer vs. Kramer* when he declares, "I don't want to live someone else's idea of how to live," and then insists, "I won't be closer to you—I won't love you more—because of a piece of paper."

The conflict resurfaces later, when Denys announces his intention to take Felicity with him on a trip, and Karen protests, nearly screeching, "Why is your freedom more important than mine?!" High on her own sanctimony, Karen lays down the law: "I won't allow it, Denys." Denys is shocked. After a pause, he whispers, "You have no idea the effect that language has on me."

Out of Africa vs. *Plenty*

In the fall of 1984, Streep temporarily moved her family to London so that she could star in *Plenty*, based on the play by David Hare and directed by Fred Schepisi. Streep would play Susan Traherne, a WWII resistance fighter who returns to England after the war and finds the world is more closed than ever to a woman who dares to demand equal treatment. Streep "loved her anger and the size of it, and her fearlessness in expressing it." She also mused, "I think we've seen lots of male heroes in drama and literature who ask a lot of their circumstances and are aggressively demanding of society and the world. I don't think that's unusual. But it's unusual when it's a woman."[q] *Plenty* (1985) was well-received but barely seen. Come Oscar time, it was essentially pushed out of the conversation by another, much bigger, war-inflected period piece featuring Streep as a woman in a male-dominated society: *Out of Africa*. *Plenty* had pedigree, but *Africa* was an event, marking, as one journalist put it, "the first-time pairing of Meryl Streep, the finest actress of her generation, and Robert Redford, the leading screen heartthrob of his generation."[r]

Why did *Out of Africa* dominate the zeitgeist while *Plenty* was all but forgotten? Oscar rules were almost surely a factor: at the time, actresses couldn't compete against themselves in the same category. Though the *Los Angeles Times* reported in December 1985 that the studios behind both films intended to campaign for the actress, "Streep's performance as author Isak Dinesen in *Out of Africa* may have the edge, since that $30 million picture figures to be seen by more people."[s] There was certainly an economic disparity between the two productions, both in terms of the budgets that went into them and in their warring messages about consumption: *Plenty* dramatized an unnameable malaise amid postwar consumerism while *Out of Africa* literally and unapologetically served as a commercial for colonialist tourism. *Out of Africa* was the kind of murky Hollywood confection that can be spun as all things to all people, feminist in that it proceeds from the point of view of a strong, independent woman but conservative in that all that woman really wants is for her boyfriend to marry her. Conversely, *Plenty* might have been too strident in its depiction of the "aggressive," "fearless" woman that Streep had so admired. But those qualities made the film ripe for reconsideration further down the line. In 2008, Molly Haskell praised *Plenty* as "one of Streep's most difficult and ambiguous" films and her "most feminist" role, adding that it was Streep's "phlegmatic good-girl reserve that gives such shocking splendor to the scenes in which she does behave outrageously."[t]

Opposite: Streep as a young
English resistence fighter
during WWII in Fred Schepisi's
Plenty (1985).

Having lost her farm, Karen
decides to leave Kenya.

Ultimately, he won't give up his utopian principles, and she won't give up any ground in what she sees as the only way to prove her worth as a woman. And so they part.

Streep bristled at this speech. "I thought it sounded like a mother admonishing her child, which did not reflect their relationship at all. It felt like a little vehicle, like a car that he could get into and slam the door and peel out in." On the day of the shoot, Streep remembers, "I said, 'All right, you know, I'm a good sport, I'll *say* it, and I'll *try* to make it work, but it won't.' And, of course, when we played it, it was the easiest and freest thing she said in the scene, because all the reason had been used up; there was nothing left to argue with but her desperation, and it was so preposterous and pathetic that it was *right*."[183]

Streep was accustomed to this feeling. In every script, she said, "there's one scene that everybody thinks, 'This is a beautiful piece, except for this one scene. This scene is fucked up, you know, they have to rewrite this.' There's always that scene, in everything I've ever done. And when you solve that, it's the Rosetta stone—it's the one that turns the understanding of the piece. I've seen it over and over… I always know, it's the one I don't want to say."[184]

Perhaps Streep should have trusted her initial instincts. Karen is making the ultimate feminist action in declaring that her own needs are equal to a man's, but as scripted and contextualized in the film, it plays as the foolish attempt of a prissy woman to clip a leash on her boyfriend. Without her speechifying, *Out of Africa* might seem more credible as an emotionally realistic portrait of a man and a woman fighting to hold on to love without conforming to age-old prescribed gender roles. Instead of merely lulling audiences with its hopelessly nostalgic fantasy, it could have held a mirror up to the time in which it was made, and the battle of the sexes in the "backlash" era. As it is, it plays as though Karen is punished for trying to contain a butterfly in a bottle, for wrecking the male fantasy that there could be such a thing as a liberated woman who supports herself financially *and* submits to sex without strings, on her partner's terms, without ever asserting what she really wants.

Selling Out

"Meryl Streep is back in top form. This means that her performance in *Out of Africa* is at the highest level of acting in film today," wrote critic Stanley Kauffmann, adding, "As was true of Brando, Streep uses her star status to risk versatility, not to sell a standard product."[185]

Standard or otherwise, *Out of Africa* proved to be an extremely successful product. In the States, it was the fifth highest grossing movie released in 1985; adjusted for inflation, it earned over $260 million worldwide. Multiple publications did colorful spreads on the film's costumes, helping to launch a safari fashion trend. Tourist agencies developed *Out of Africa* packages to capitalize on rich Westerners' sudden interest in the region. It was the first Meryl Streep film to not only ignite popular and intellectual culture, but to become a commercial phenomenon in venues completely divorced from movies. This success came as a shock to Streep herself, who admitted that when she first saw *Africa*, she cried—not because the film was so emotional, but because she thought it was destined to flop. "Frankly," Streep admitted in 1986, "I was surprised by how many regular people seemed to care about that woman in *Out of Africa* as well as that film."[186]

But *Out of Africa* was the Academy's idea of "quality." It was undeniably a throwback to the kinds of movies Hollywood used to make, which must have been appealing to a notoriously nostalgic voting body. At the Oscar ceremony on March 24, 1986 (cohosted by Jane Fonda), *Africa* took home several major awards, including screenplay, director, and picture. When F. Murray Abraham ripped open the best actress envelope, he exclaimed, "I consider this woman the greatest actress in the English language"—causing some watching to assume the winner was Streep, who had already been billed as such by many. Then he announced that the winner was Geraldine Page, nominated for *The Trip to Bountiful* (1985). Streep leapt to her feet and applauded.

One thing the film was not was a feminist phenomenon, and in fact some of its harshest criticism came from women. Gossip columnist Liz Smith reported that in Denmark, Streep's accent "has become something of a national joke."[187] Pauline Kael, as per usual, led the pack of negative reviews, although she didn't place the blame solely on her favorite blond punching bag: "Streep is animated in the early scenes, but Redford doesn't give out anything for her to play against, and the energy goes out of her performance." Kael also picked on the scene that had given Streep qualms: "When she demands that he marry her, it's as if a couple of pages from a bad novel about a possessive woman had been pasted into the middle of a *National Geographic* photo essay."[188]

Ms. magazine's Molly Haskell declared that Streep's best effort wasn't enough to save a doomed enterprise, in which the characters "seem defanged, domesticated, turned into models of safari chic and PBS liberalism […]." While Haskell allowed that Streep's accent was "plausible," her best efforts weren't enough to overcome "a fundamental, temperamental clash: Streep's ego (and genius) as an actress is to submit completely to another character; Dinesen's was to assert, rule, behave outrageously, in order to become, completely, herself. To portray her faithfully demands an act of exposure of which Streep, for all her talents, is incapable."[189]

Was Meryl Streep miscast in *Out of Africa*? The impression you get of her Karen Blixen is that she was an uptight European whose sensual proclivities were unlocked by the hot, savage climes of Africa—exactly the kind of facile "America abroad" perspective that Redford said he hoped the film would avoid. Today *Africa* represents the peak of Streep's early fame—and, at least for the moment, there was nowhere to go but down. Ironically for a film that functions best as a fantasy travelogue, it's the film that brought Streep's career down to earth, revealing her limitations as an actress and her mortality as a star.

After Africa

For all the angst of the shoot, the Streep/Gummer family had found in Africa a kind of idyll. "In Kenya when we woke we looked out the window at Mount Kilimanjaro floating in mist," Streep recalled. "And I thought, 'After this, can we really go back to Eighty-seventh Street, where the only place the kids can play is in a park full of dog poop and diesel exhaust?'"[190]

Celebrity wasn't getting any easier; even in seen-it-all Manhattan, her very presence caused a commotion. "I think this is what turns public figures into alcoholics," she mused. "You really have to do something when people are watching you all day long." And so in August 1985 the Gummer family moved into a secluded $1.8 million estate in Connecticut, complete with a massive art studio for Don. "What we really bought was privacy," Streep said. "A house that can't be seen from the road."

Connecticut would remain the Gummer family home base through the end of the century, but Streep would soon sojourn in what was still unchartered territory for her: Hollywood.

The success of *Out of Africa* came as a surprise to Meryl Streep, who thought it would surely bomb.

6

Madeline Ashton

Death Becomes Her (1992)
Robert Zemeckis

"In a season where most of the female leads are prostitutes, there's not going to be a lot of work for women over forty. Like hookers, actresses seem to lose their market appeal around that age."[191]
—Meryl Streep, 1992

After *Out of Africa*, for the first time Streep struggled to maintain her stardom and esteem in the face of a changing industry, her own advancing age, the demands of her family (with the birth of daughters Grace and Louisa, the Gummers had four kids by 1991), and her increasingly open frustration with the paucity of opportunities for women. Sydney Pollack's Oscar-winning epic led to a tidal wave of criticism against her. The most frequent complaints: Unlike other top movie stars of the 1980s—the Cruises, the Stallones—she never seemed to play "herself," and thus didn't have a consistent brand to offer from film to film. She had too much technique—you could *see* her acting. There was no "there" to her performances, the only thing tying them together being the sense they had been planned intellectually rather than felt organically. Perhaps most bruising: now that she commanded $4 million a picture—nowhere near what comparable male stars earned, but a lot for a woman—she was overpaid. Yes, she netted nine Oscar nominations in eighteen movies. But, "national treasure or no," as the industry mag *Premiere* put it in 1992, "Streep still cannot open a film."[192]

Streep didn't help her cause by choosing a number of wanly received and/or financially underperforming vehicles. Some, like *Ironweed* (1987) and *A Cry in the Dark* (1988), backed up her "no fun" rep. Other films, particularly the comedies *She-Devil* (1989) and *Defending Your Life* (1991), suggested a concerted effort to change her persona, a perception Streep added to when she moved her family to Los Angeles in 1990.

In many of these films Streep in some way explored the struggle adult women face to live up to expectations, to maintain appearances in the most literal of senses. *Heartburn* (1986), *Postcards from the Edge* (1990), and *She-Devil* were particularly confrontational and self-aware regarding the challenges and paradoxes of aging, which Streep herself felt, as a woman and, particularly, as a famous actress. In 1989, in the middle of this run, Streep turned forty. She'd later admit that the birthday sparked a bout of soul-searching, given that in the eyes of her industry, "Once women passed childbearing age they could only be seen as grotesque on some level."[193]

The drift away from serious prestige pictures into lower-brow comedy, the move to Los Angeles, and the sense that, as a woman in Hollywood, her clock was ticking—all of these factors came together most successfully in *Death Becomes Her*, Robert Zemeckis's 1992 horror farce about "the living dead in Beverly Hills," starring Streep as a vain actress who, driven mad by competition between women in a toxic industry town, embraces the secret to eternal youth, damn the consequences. Dismissed by contemporary critics, in the States it grossed just slightly more than its inflated budget—which was still enough to make it the biggest hit of a period in which Streep and popular audiences fell out of sync. Seen today, the film is startlingly reflective of its time—and of the premature midlife crisis Streep was battling behind the scenes.

Death by Heartburn

Streep's transition to lighter fare began with a reunion with her *Silkwood* writer (Nora Ephron) and director (Mike Nichols). *Heartburn*, based on Ephron's novel about her own marriage to Carl Bernstein, allowed Streep to dip a toe into comic dialogue and situations within what was still essentially a drama, a blend that she had long wanted to attempt. But *Heartburn* bombed; the movie itself generated less interest than the affair that Streep was rumored to be having with costar Jack Nicholson. Such rumors were probably false, but at least they added a much-needed dose of spice to Streep's persona.

By 1988, the question posed in an essay by Mike Hammer was "Is Meryl Streep ever going to lighten up?" Hammer boiled down the issue to Streep's choice of roles. "While such movies as *Plenty* and *Ironweed* were dramatically demanding for Streep, an actress who likes to take risks, they are not appealing to moviegoing audiences. And the woman who is universally acclaimed as one of the leading actresses of our time suddenly finds herself in an unenviable

Meryl Streep tries her hand at comedy in Robert Zemeckis's *Death Becomes Her* (1992), in which she plays Madeline Ashton.

Top: Madeline, an actress whose career is slowing down, performs in a tacky musical based on Tennessee Williams's *Sweet Bird of Youth*.

Bottom: After her show, Madeline greets her old friend Helen (Goldie Hawn), who is with her fiancé, Ernest (Bruce Willis).

situation. At a time in her career when she reportedly makes an estimated $4 million per film, her box office appeal is waning." She might be the greatest actress of her generation, but "audiences are staying home."[194]

Her choice of roles during this period was complicated by a major project that didn't happen. Streep had lobbied hard for, and landed, the lead in Oliver Stone's adaptation of *Evita*. Then, in September 1989, two months before recording was scheduled to begin, she suddenly dropped out, citing "exhaustion," although it later came to light there had been a salary dispute that soured her on the production. "I can work very, very hard, but not when I feel I'm being lied to, or that I mistrust the circumstances," Streep said cryptically that December. "It was a bitter disappointment," she added, "But it's just a movie. As Albert [Brooks] said, 'You know, Meryl, you could do this and it would be the toughest thing you've ever done in your life. […] And everyone would say, So what?' […] That's the joke about me, that I do all these really hard roles." She laughed, at herself as much as at the notion of being punished for being too good at her job. "I guess they're sick of me."[195] Later, when Madonna got the part in Alan Parker's film version (1996), Streep was less sanguine. "I could rip her throat out," she blurted. "I can sing better than she can, if that counts for anything."[196]

Going Hollywood

Streep had been "looking for a script that made me laugh," but she felt distanced from Hollywood's idea of "comedy": "I go to a lot of movies where people are all around me laughing and I feel like I'm from outerspace because I find it dangerous and stupid and horrible and degrading to women and all these things."[197] She would become particularly annoyed by the success of prostitute comedy *Pretty Woman* in 1990. "I am upset that fifteen-year-old girls want to go see that four and five times," she admitted.[198] She turned forty in 1989, while living in the capital of the film industry—a city where, as one piece on Streep put it, "liposuction is fast becoming as popular as the convertible and teen-age visits to the plastic surgeon are estimated to be up threefold in the 1980s."[199] She felt the difference immediately. "I was offered within one year three different witch roles," she'd say later. "Three different witches in three different contexts. It was almost like the world was saying—or the studios were saying—'We don't know what to do with you.'"[200]

Postcards and *She-Devil*, the two films Streep would make around her fortieth birthday, would turn a comic mirror on the objectification of women, reflecting, as Streep put it, her own experience of "how you can be beaten up in Hollywood because of the way you look."[201] The Gummer family migrated to Los Angeles so Streep could shoot the movies—her first projects to actually film in Hollywood, which Streep had only previously visited for awards ceremonies. It was supposed to be a temporary trip, but the work kept coming. After an afternoon spent at Albert Brooks's swimming pool, she signed on to make another comedy, *Defending Your Life*. In May 1990, the Gummers finally gave in and bought a $3 million mansion in Brentwood, just west of Beverly Hills.

Neither *Postcards* nor *She-Devil* was successful enough to match Streep's culture-defining hits of the early eighties, and by 1990, she was increasingly plagued by the perception that she was out of touch with the public. "The question about audiences turning away from me is… interesting," Streep admitted in 1990, although she went on to deflect the blame from herself and her own choices: "Audiences are shrinking. As the marketing strategy defines more and more narrowly who they want to reach—males from 16 to 25—it's become a chicken-and-egg syndrome. Which came first? First, they release all these summer movies, then do a demographic survey of who's going to see them."[202]

By spring of 1991, when Streep switched agencies—leaving the New York–based ICM for the *très* Hollywood Creative Artists Agency (CAA)—gossip columnist Liz Smith was not alone in perceiving the move as a sign that "the great Meryl 'went Hollywood,'" while also suffering something like a midlife crisis. "There are those who say Meryl has changed a lot," Smith wrote. "Her last few films have not been big at the box office and she is fretting over having passed the 40 mark—the 'problem age' for actresses. One who seems to know says: 'She has gone from being legendary to being difficult.'"[203]

Smith might as well have been describing Madeline Ashton, the aging actress Streep played in her first film after signing on to new management.

Forever Young?

The first frames of *Death Becomes Her* wink at Streep's devalued stardom. Before she appears on-screen, we see unsatisfied customers streaming out of a Broadway show, a discarded *Playbill* with her face on it drowning in a puddle. Cut to a heavily made-up Streep as Madeline, star of a misbegotten musical production of Tennessee Williams's *Sweet Bird of Youth*, singing to her reflection in a stage mirror: "What do I see? That's the question I'm really afraid of." Soon she breaks into a lavish dance number, slinkily hoofing her heart out while singing about her fractured identity as "actress, woman, star and lover, sister, sweetheart, slave and mother." As Madeline, here Streep is parodying the impossible hand dealt to many adult women—be all things to all people, at work and at home, and do it with a smile on your face—by literalizing it. Judging by the crowds streaming out of the theater—and the horrified face of Helen (Goldie Hawn), a mousey book editor who's come to see her college frenemy Madeline's big show—the specter of a woman confronting her own objectification and struggling to live up to expectations is the antithesis of entertainment.

But to Helen's date, Ernest (Bruce Willis, under layers of dehunkifying hair and makeup), a plastic surgeon whose bread and butter is providing temporary salves to female insecurity, "She's sensational!"

The film jumps ahead several years. Ernest has left Helen for Madeline, and Helen has turned into a grotesquely obese shut-in. Sent to a mental ward, she realizes that the only way to heal herself is by getting revenge. We jump ahead again: a decade into their marriage, Madeline and Ernest are miserable. She's become a plastic surgery addict in an effort to stall the slippage of her acting career; he's become a drunk and, his own once-promising surgical career abandoned, a mortician to the stars. The pair accept an invitation to a party for Helen's new book— *Forever Young*—so that Madeline can gloat at the sight of her fat "friend." But surprise, surprise: the fifty-something Helen somehow looks younger— and thinner—than ever. And she's intent on getting Ernest back.

Driven mad by the preternatural youthfulness of her rival, Madeline flees to the gothic mansion of underground beauty merchant Lisle (Isabella Rossellini). A dish in a barely-there sarong, topless but for rings of necklaces covering her nipples, Lisle swears she's seventy-one. "Screw the natural law!" Lisle declares, offering Madeline a pricey potion that she promises "stops the aging process dead in its tracks, and forces it into retreat […] don't drink it, and continue to watch yourself rot." Madeline drinks it, of course, and her face and body are transformed before her (and our) eyes. Lisle claims there are only two caveats: Madeline must promise to withdraw from public life in ten years, so that no one gets suspicious about her eternal youth; and, Lisle warns, "Take care of your body."

She doesn't, and the movie spins into all-out, technologically-enabled horror-farce, as Madeline discovers that Helen is also a Lisle client, the two women realize they're both walking corpses that will start to decay if injured in any way, and Ernest attempts to flee, lest he be forced into using his mortician skills to maintain the visages of these lady zombies for the rest of time. Ultimately, the women find themselves in a Sartrean hell for self-loathing women—doomed to keep each other company for eternity.

In plot, performance, blocking, design, and lighting, *Death* is decidedly cartoonish, a self-aware spoof-riff on *Bride of Frankenstein* (1935) and *Alice in Wonderland* (1951), with a glaze of soap and a core of drawing room comedy. Coscreenwriter David Koepp described it as "how *Night of the Living Dead* [1968] would have turned out if Noel Coward had written it."[204] To Streep, it "was a documentary about the Los Angeles fixation with aging,"[205] as well as an acidic indictment of superficial competition between women, which she described as "the only issue for women, from age eleven until they, I guess, hit fifty and don't give a damn anymore."[206]

Streep still gave a damn. The film reflected her real anxiety that the natural process of aging was a no-no in her chosen career: "I don't want the choice to be, 'Get carved, or you don't work!'" When a reporter asked if she had succumbed to the pressure to artificially enhance her beauty, Streep began to gesture toward her temples, then quickly retracted her hand. "Well, I've had… braces and things." She then admitted, "I was ordered by this company to get a trainer; I just had a baby, so they had reason to worry about my midsection. I don't normally do that."[207] Forced onto a treadmill for the first time in her life, Streep ran seven miles every day to get Madeline's post-potion perfect bod.

Indeed, it's the most physical performance Streep had yet committed to screen, all broad weeping, smirking, and eye-rolling. Much of the film is surprisingly talky, with no mystery to the performances, because nothing is withheld. But performative subtlety may not have jibed with the over-the-top, state-of-the-art special effects that were the marketing hook of the movie.

Streep loved the role-swapping nature of the casting: sexy Goldie Hawn playing a lifelong wallflower, notoriously cerebral Meryl going vamp. (Hawn at that time was a box office star who longed to be taken seriously, while Meryl had Oscars but couldn't buy a hit.) But as she so often did, Streep suggested the script needed work. "Meryl was interested in playing Madeline as a real person, to understand why she behaves the way she does, the weakness beneath it," said Koepp, who agreed to rewrite material concerning Madeline's affair with a young stud, which she felt was unrealistically male in its point of view. "She proposed it might be more real and heartbreaking if Madeline really tried to convince herself that it means more than it does," Koepp said. "She was right: we'd gone for the cheap laugh by having her be a bitch, instead of a real one showing she's human."[208]

Streep got into character by "thinking about being just slightly pissed off all the time. Madeline is irritated at everything: time passing, everything falling down and having no control over it. And there's enough in my day to feed that."[209] This seems like an oblique reference to the way the film's reliance on technology got in the way of her process. "Whatever concentration you can apply to that kind of comedy is just shredded," she'd say later. "You stand there like a piece of machinery—

Desperate to restore her youth, Madeline calls on the services of Lisle von Rhuman (Isabella Rossellini), who sells her a mysterious potion.

Opposite, top: When Madeline and Helen learn they've both taken Lisle's potion, their rivalry escalates to violence.

Opposite, bottom: The undead Madeline relies on the services of her husband, a plastic surgeon turned mortician, to maintain the illusion of physical perfection.

For the first and last time in her career, Streep took part in a film that uses special effects throughout.

Following pages: From then on, Madeline and Helen are prisoners in a shared hell, that of eternal youth with just a few conditions.

they should get machinery to do it."[210] Ironically, Doug Smythe, the computer artist in charge of syncing the "morphing" effect that would achieve the transition between old Madeline and young, marveled at how quickly Streep adapted to the process: "Meryl is the closest we've come to finding a motion-controllable person. Her ability to remember what she did physically on previous takes—down to very precise actions—was amazingly accurate."[211]

Zemeckis, a pioneer in the art of previsual-ization, was tightly wedded to storyboards, meaning there was little room between the tedious blocking and replication of labor for the kind of play Streep enjoyed. The scenes requiring the most elaborate effects—like the one in which Madeline's head becomes turned around backward—had to be shot first, so that the effects house would have time to work on the shots. The effects are convincing, but sometimes Streep's performance isn't; when her head is on backward, she's supposed to be having a face-to-face conversation with Willis's character, but her eyes look glazed over, as though the actress couldn't figure out how to pretend they were being filmed in the same room.

"It is really hard to dive into elaborate special effects work before you really have a handle on the movie," Zemeckis acknowledged. And this was Streep's first experience with such technology. She was joined in her performance by a living

body double and also eight animatronic Meryl Streep stunt puppets. For the replicas, Streep had to submit to having her face cast, a process she described as "sort of horrifying."[212]

Making matters worse, the makeup crew soon learned that because Streep's skin was so sensitive and prone to allergies, she would need the prosthetics designed to age her by ten years reapplied in the middle of the day, and ultimately new glues and application techniques were developed in order to accommodate her. She made the most of it, said makeup artist Kevin Haney: "Meryl used the makeup to help her perform the character; she would move differently, her gestures and expressions would change—she essentially became another person right there."[213] But Streep repeatedly pushed for minimization of the makeup. "They kept making me look 70," she complained, "and it's gotta be 54."[214] It was almost as if Hollywood didn't know what a middle-aged woman looked like.

All told, it was a seven-month shoot—the longest of Streep's career. She had mixed feelings about the experience. "I wanted to feel au courant, like I was part of the current movie-making style," Streep said, "but I'm not sure I'd sign up for another film like this, because it can be tedious with all the special effects, the machines and the computer…"[215] Eight years later, she was less diplomatic, calling it "my first, my last, my only" special effects film. "I loved how it turned out.

Feeling that she had been typecast based on her "serious face,"[u] in the late 1980s to early 1990s Meryl Streep consciously attempted to pick lighter material. Her first out-and-out comedic role came in *She-Devil* (1989), a wild, tacky-bordering-on-surrealistic satire set in a virtually dystopian battleground of the sexes. Streep starred as a glamorous romance novelist who steals the weaselly husband, Bob (Ed Begley Jr.), of a frumpy wreck, Ruth Patchett (Roseanne Barr). Streep, ever up for a challenge, originally wanted the Roseanne part; director Susan Seidelman was relieved when she agreed to play bombshell Mary instead. "Even though Roseanne is not as experienced as an actor," Seidelman said, "it would have been less effective if a glamorous

woman was frumping it up."[v] Streep saw her character as a parody of Hollywood's nipped-and-tucked, peroxide-blond, absurdly unrealistic standard of beauty. "I thought I was making fun of that. But I must say, the crew treated me real nice when I had my Mary outfit on, and my fingernails were all false and pasted on, and I had all this sloppy jewelry, and my hair teased up and fluffed, and the makeup was on like lacquer. Barbie is never going to go out of style." She added that there was "nothing wrong" with actresses conforming to that superficial ideal—"unless there are no other women in movies. I don't want to ride a polemic here, but I do like people to see the beauty in the soul."[w] *She-Devil* would land with a thud. Though Streep attracted some good reviews (for Vincent Canby, her performance was "almost

worth the price of admission. Emphasize the 'almost'"[x]), audiences were indifferent. Streep saw the film as a good-faith attempt to step out of her comfort zone, and it also spoke to gender issues that meant something to her; its failure hurt. Months after the film was released, she spoke of *She-Devil* defensively. "I was conscious of needing to work and there was nothing to do," she said. "So I did that. I wasn't pregnant, and I wanted to work. I loved *She-Devil* but in the mix, it didn't work."[y]

Opposite: Mary Fisher,
a famous author played by
Streep in *She-Devil* (1989),
directed by Susan Seidelman.

In *Death Becomes Her*, the
special effects even manage
to turn Madeline's head
around 180 degrees.

But it's not fun to act to a lampstand. 'Pretend this is Goldie, right here!' Uh, no, I'm sorry, Bob, she went off the mark by five centimeters, and now her head won't match her neck! It was like being at the dentist."[216]

The film, Streep would say, "was in advance of its time." In its time, reviews were vicious. "This is a movie that hates women," declared Richard Corliss in *Time*, dismissing *Death* as "*She-Devil* with a makeover."[217] Corliss didn't elaborate on his claim of misogyny, but other critics suggested the film's sociopolitical failure lay in its plot about two bitchy women fighting over one dull man. This is a misreading: Helen and Madeline clearly only care about Ernest as a manifestation of their competition with each other, which is itself a symptom of the world the movie critiques—Hollywood—which offers so few opportunities that one woman's gain becomes another woman's automatic loss. Think of how Streep reacted to Madonna's casting in *Evita*—even after Streep herself backed out of the project.

The female response was different. *Death Becomes Her* grossed $15.2 million in its first five days—or about what *She-Devil* had made in its entire theatrical run—and females constituted fifty-six percent of the opening night audience. "If a woman had made this movie I'd probably read it as a daring portrayal of female rage and rebellion," wrote Ella Taylor in the *LA Weekly*. As it was, she praised Zemeckis for giving his actresses a chance to invert their images, resulting in "a portrayal of aging women that's as vicious as any I've ever seen. They're so over the top that you can't possibly see them as anything but a send-up of a culture whose obsessive search for youth and beauty has rendered it utterly grotesque—and, perhaps unwittingly, a comment on what middle-aged actresses have to do to stay in the game."[218] Still, Streep's comedy phase was deemed by all but her to be a failure. A few years later, when a reporter suggested that *Death* in particular was beneath her, she snapped sarcastically, "I'm so sorry you think that," adding, "Everything I do is serious even, as you said, my lighter things. To me, they were very serious. I mean even the hyperbolic comedies like *Death Becomes Her*. Sure, I don't think anybody took it that way, but I liked what it was about."[219]

Its central issue—the pressure on women to stall the aging process—remained at the front of her mind. "I know movies are a function of our dream world. And when you project yourself on screen, it's easier to project yourself into what you were, not what you are […]." She sighed. "Movies are a young person's playground."[220]

She admitted that she was "horribly disappointed" that "people don't see what I consider some of my best work. But I know that I have a video life. Most of my fans are home with their children waiting for my films to come out on video."[221] In defeat, she was working to move

Lisle tries to give Ernest the potion that will make him eternally young, but he won't have it.

Opposite: Though Ernest wishes to escape from Lisle's, Helen and Madeline try again to convince him to drink the potion. But faced with the possibility of immortality and being with them forever, Ernest falls from the roof of the castle and leaves the two women behind.

away from her perch as the rarefied goddess of acting, casting herself as the voice of the housewife everywoman. She would continue this positioning years later, when she insisted she was unaware of the "backlash" directed at her leading up to *Death Becomes Her*. Dismissing criticism that the Gummers settled in Los Angeles "because I was desperate to revive my career that was flagging," Streep insisted, "If it was flagging, I didn't know it." They bought the mansion in Brentwood, she maintained, because her son Henry had bopped between six schools on four continents in his seven years, and he finally said, "Mom, I don't want to move anymore."[222]

Streep's concern for her kids was surely genuine, but to suggest she had no idea that her career was "flagging" contradicts many statements that, as we've seen, she made at the time, up to and including a speech she made to a Screen Actor's Guild conference in which she declared her frustration with the roles available to her. This period marked Streep's brashest, most public show of feminism to date, and that the actress would later diffuse her hot-button, unpopular displays of ambition and activism through the prism of motherhood suggests just how tightly she still held to the gender-normative lessons of her youth. Three years after *Death Becomes Her*, she'd finally take on an on-screen role that mirrored the role she'd taken in the press—that of "just" a housewife.

7

Francesca Johnson

The Bridges of Madison County (1995)
Clint Eastwood

"It was easy for me to become prominent, and I didn't have anything to do with that. The difficulty is in maintaining a life's work and making it interesting, constantly reinventing it, challenging myself—and to remain open as an actor and to keep pushing the boulder uphill."[223]
—Meryl Streep, 1995

In 1994, Streep's Hollywood experiment came to an end. Spooked by an earthquake and bothered by the local custom of intermingling social life and work—a.k.a. schmoozing—Streep moved her family back to Connecticut. Again, she chalked it up to parental strategy: "If my children went to high school on the West Coast, that's where they'd go to college."[224] But in Hollywood, it was perceived as a retreat, an admission that her effort to shake her career up, by lightening up, hadn't worked. "She went from being a great classical actress to playing parts in Hollywood that others could have done," said Alan Pakula that year. "Sometimes they put her into a picture and it's like having this huge motor on this tiny car."[225]

An example of such questionable use of Streep's talents was the 1994 white-water rafting drama *The River Wild*. The last film Streep made before leaving Los Angeles, it seemed like a final "if you can't beat 'em, join 'em" gambit. Having complained futilely about Hollywood's obsession with action movies fronted by rock-hard men, she now went with the flow, taking on a punishing exercise and diet regime to transform herself into the shape of a hero. The film was a modest hit, but not blockbuster enough to justify a new phase as an action star. Once it failed to set the world on fire, Streep went back to basics.

That move served her well. Streep's biggest hit of the 1990s was *The Bridges of Madison County*, an austere, unhurried two-hander period romance about a brief affair between two strangers, based on the best-selling book by Robert James Waller. As Francesca, an Italian war bride turned quietly bitter, a middle-aged housewife disillusioned with life in rural Iowa twenty years into her marriage to a former GI, Streep imbues an adulterous woman with sympathetic intelligence and angst.

The story of a frustrated woman who comes to know herself through explorations outside the home came at an interesting time for Streep. Though the actress continued to steadfastly deny

responsibility for any kind of professional savvy, as journalist Rachel Abramowitz put it, "no one seemed to believe her when she stated that she had made a number of career decisions based on the welfare of her four children."[226] Streep was miffed by a 1994 *New York Times* article in which the testimony of an unnamed "friend" was used to discredit the actress's claims that "her eyes glaze over when deals and contracts are discussed," instead suggesting that Streep "is a shrewd businesswoman with the ambition of earning as much money as possible."[227]

In hindsight, it seems like Streep's public positioning of herself as a harried wife and mother, and her downplaying of her identity as a careerist or feminist, was owed in part to her adolescent understanding that "opinions weren't attractive" in a man's world. But her protestations also aligned her with an audience of women, the grown-up versions of the girls she knew in high school "who waited for things to happen to them," the mothers who were "home with their children waiting for my films to come out on video." Again, we could surmise that she was taking a lesson in what not to do from someone like Jane Fonda, who had presented herself as the face of progressive Hollywood and thus engendered suspicion from audiences who didn't approve of her politics. Streep's choices instead seemed to embody the notion that the way to enact change was not to craft sermons that would be heard only by the choir, but to deliver potentially subversive messages to the everyday, nonpoliticized people who most needed to hear them by sneaking those ideas into their entertainment. *Bridges*, like most of Streep's early successes, is a work of historical fiction, in which Streep opens up a new way of looking at a time period merely by embodying a feminine perspective from within it. A film that took seriously the internal life of a housewife gave voice to the otherwise voiceless—itself a political action.

Transforming Soap Into Sirk

Streep was well aware that *Bridges* offered her a unique opportunity. As an actress of a certain age, she said, "You're limited by the number of scripts you're appropriate for in a year. There are not 27, there are not 7. Sometimes there are none. Most of

For the role of Francesca Johnson in Clint Eastwood's *The Bridges of Madison County*, Meryl Streep would draw inspiration from Anna Magnani.

This page and opposite: Alone for a few days while her husband and children are away, Francesca Johnson decides to go around with a photographer, Robert Kincaid (Clint Eastwood), who asks her for directions.

the women in movies are sex objects, what my father calls 'scantily clad,' and they are there to be dumped, humped, maimed, or killed—a victim or an appendage. I always say to my kids, 'Read, read—why don't you read?' All the conflicted, interesting characters are in literature."[228]

For a lot of Americans in 1995, particularly women, *The Bridges of Madison County* was what passed for "literature." Short and floridly written, the book had been a best seller for almost three years by the time the film was released. Tourists flocked to the rural area of Iowa described in the novel, seeking inspiration for their own romances. Advice columnist Ann Landers was overwhelmed with letters asking why the book's female character ultimately chose her stifling life as a housewife over running away with her lover.

But Meryl Streep wasn't a fan. She dismissed the book as "a crime against literature"; she couldn't even get through it.[229] And yet, when Clint Eastwood called her at home and asked her to read the screenplay, she did. "The novel was written from the man's perspective," Eastwood said later. "We preferred to tell the story through the woman's point of view."[230] Streep was duly impressed. "One of the things that made me nuts in the book is that the woman was invisible," Streep said. "I couldn't picture her in any way with any specificity. But this person

that [screenwriter Richard LaGravenese] had conceived was very visible to me."[231]

Still, she wondered: "Why does Clint Eastwood want to do this piece of material? It's a woman's book. Any number of actors would run away. And here's the King of Cool wanting to open up his soul."[232]

Eastwood had signed on first to star, and then stepped in as director when Bruce Beresford dropped out. As an actor, he could relate to the character of Robert Kincaid, a drifter/stranger who is both critical of the American myth of domestic bliss and covetous of its comforts. As a director, he was drawn to the challenge of producing an old-fashioned romance, consisting primarily of two people talking, in an MTV era. Though he mentioned John Ford and Howard Hawks as aesthetic inspirations, the filmmaker Eastwood's *Bridges* would most call to mind was Douglas Sirk. Hollywood's poet of midcentury forbidden love, Sirk had frequently used illicit romances to comment on the inherent conservatism of the postwar era—what Eastwood's character would refer to as "this 'American family' ethic that seems to have hypnotized the country."

A Return to Her Roots

Streep signed on just two weeks before *Bridges* started shooting in September 1994. She had

dropped the fitness regimes that had been mandated by her two previous films, allowing her body to soften into a more natural shape, and her rounder frame fit the character. "I thought it added a certain reality," she'd say, noting that Francesca, like Meryl, "was fully who she was at her age."[233] Her body presented a challenge for costume designer Colleen Kelsall, who had been instructed by Eastwood to outfit the actress in housedresses, and not the T-shirts and jeans the character wore in the book. "We wanted Meryl to look sexy, but not in the traditional sense," said Kelsall. "Women of that period were voluptuous. We cinched her belts a wee bit too tight to make you think of those Italian film stars of that era like Sophia Loren, who wore those tatty little *schmates* with tight belts and looked like she'd been sweating."[234]

Streep reportedly took inspiration not from Loren, but from another midcentury Italian star, Anna Magnani, viewing Pier Paolo Pasolini's *Mamma Roma* (1962) before the shoot. As Francesca, her accent and vocal cadences were not as exaggerated as Magnani's in Pasolini's film; for the first time, Streep's accent acted like a transparent gloss, changing the effect of her own voice but not transforming it entirely. Her performance mainly resembles Magnani's in its physicality. Her Francesca is a heavy presence, strong but exceedingly feminine. Streep also borrows Magnani's gift for blending pathos with

physical comedy, screwing up her face and gesturing with her arms as she talks, remaining deadpan as she drops unexpected wisecracks into otherwise serious conversation. The overall effect is both earthy and unusual, befitting a character who was both outsider and everywoman, who transgresses the propriety of the home but ultimately sacrifices her own happiness for the good of her family.

Streep's lack of prep time suited Eastwood's approach to production; he wanted his star to go in as a blank slate and have an experience on camera. He planned to shoot in sequence, "so that the actors' relationship could develop as naturally as the characters."[235] Director and actress barely knew each other the night she showed up at a pub in Des Moines for a party kicking off the production. Streep brought her three-year-old daughter Louisa along in case she needed an excuse to leave early. That night, Eastwood unnerved his actress with a warning: "I hope you're not going to do a big accent thing." Streep remembered, "I was afraid to do an accent ever again in my life—they jump on me so for it. [But] there was no way Francesca wasn't going to have an accent. It was organic to how I saw the character." Worried, she slept fitfully. "The next day I was going to have to open my mouth and *speak* for the first time."[236]

The next day, they rehearsed Francesca and Robert's first meeting. When Streep spoke

Francesca's first words to Robert—"Are you supposed to be in Iowa?"—Eastwood, in character as Kincaid, heard her accent for the first time. To his own surprise, Eastwood was fine with it. Not that he told her so. "He didn't really speak to me for the first half of the film, and I was getting alarmed," Streep admitted. Finally, one day he said, "You know, I don't say much unless I don't like it."[237]

Eastwood would prove to be the hands-off, no-fuss director of Streep's dreams. He felt his job, "beside picking a script, is casting the right people. But then after that, the real responsibility is to make those people feel at home. Set an atmosphere where everybody is extremely relaxed and there's no tension. Coming from acting, you know what rattles people, what rattles you."[238]

Even better for Streep, within that relaxed environment Eastwood gave her room to play, to discover things in the moment, and he knew when to say when. "He may just shoot rehearsal and move," she quickly realized. "He is not going to explore this 40 times."[239] Improvisation was encouraged; sometimes Eastwood would break character in front of the camera and, as he put it, "ask them to say something other than what had been planned, to change the lines."[240] For Streep, it felt like a theater piece, one that reminded her of her roots, before she got used to the laconic pace of typical moviemaking. "You know, people have called me a technical actor," she mused. "But I have always loved that first encounter. I almost always like the first reading better than anything we ever do subsequently. I come ready and I don't want to screw around and waste the first 10 takes on adjusting lighting and everybody else getting comfortable."[241]

Streep, said Eastwood, "didn't have time to think, she couldn't do anything but concentrate on her character and play it, nothing else."[242]

Historical Fiction

The story of the Francesca/Robert romance, occurring over four days in 1965, is framed by scenes set in the present. Francesca has just died, and Michael (Victor Slezak) and Carolyn (Annie Corley), her adult son and daughter, have returned to the Iowa farmhouse where they grew up for the reading of their mother's will. She's left them journals, describing and defending the brief affair that changed her life.

In the film, this framing device is regrettably executed (in its stilted acting and cringe-worthy expository dialogue, it suggests the downside of Eastwood's hands-off directorial style) but narratively productive. At the beginning of the film, Carolyn and Michael, both married themselves, speak of their mother disparagingly. When they find out that Francesca's request to have her ashes thrown off one of Madison County's bridges replicates Robert's final wishes,

Michael exclaims, "Damn him! I knew Mom wouldn't have thought of that herself!" They can't seem to fathom that their square mom could have had an internal life at all, let alone a passionate one, and assume that this mysterious stranger who came to town in 1965 must have forced himself on her. As if anticipating this reaction, she has defended herself in a letter: "As one gets older, one's fears subside," she writes to her kids. "What becomes most important is to be known." The framing device aligns Francesca's story and her method of telling it with the traditional ways in which the female perspective on history has been disseminated: through letters and diaries passed down first to family and friends and then potentially to a larger, institutionally approved audience, through which personal/social history could become retold as just plain history.

Subtextually, this device prepares the viewer to understand that Francesca and Robert's story is more than a romance—it's a work of fiction that, in its depiction of a very specific time and place, serves as a micro-focused, localized stand-in for a perspective on a much bigger historical moment. Francesca's kids are first skeptical, then ultimately sympathetic to their mother's story; they feel betrayed, but in that betrayal they're forced to confront their assumptions about the "American dream." This is a mirror of the magic that Streep works on viewers—winning them over to a new perspective through emotional response, converting unlikely audiences to progressive understandings through focus on the personal rather than the overtly political.

When the film cuts into flashback, showing Francesca housekeeping on the day that her kids and husband leave for a state fair (thus opening up a space in her life for a dashing stranger), the perspective abruptly shifts from Francesca's aghast adult children to that of Francesca herself. Aged forty-five, twenty years removed from the town of Bari where she grew up and where her husband wooed her at the end of World War II, she has become an invisible presence in a land that's not her own. Her kids and husband rely on her labor, but they barely see her and have nothing to say to her. She's like a piece of machinery that makes their lives run without them ever having to think about it.

The next day, *National Geographic* photographer Robert Kincaid shows up at her farm seeking directions, and she decides it would be easier to ride with him to the covered bridge he seeks to photograph, rather than explain how to get there. It's not like she has much else to do: "I was just going to have some iced tea and then, uh, split the atom," she cracks dryly. "But that could wait."

It's a sweltering summer day, and when they arrive back at her house, Francesca invites Robert in for iced tea. He ultimately stays for dinner, and over many beers, the two exchange

If aliens had invaded the planet during the summer of 1990, when the culture was ruled by movies like *Total Recall, Dick Tracy,* and *Pretty Woman* in which the main roles for actresses were as duplicitous plot devices and/or ladies of the night, the extraterrestrials might have assumed—as Meryl Streep put it in her keynote speech at the Screen Actors Guild National Women's Conference that August—that "the chief occupation of women on Earth was hooking, and I don't mean rugs."[z]

Streep made these remarks, critical of the industry that employed her, in the middle of a difficult stretch of her own career—at age forty-one, she was struggling to find solid leading roles that reflected her own interests and values without turning off mainstream audiences—that coincided with a particularly arid period for studio films with substantial roles for women. In 1989 women played only 29% of all roles in Hollywood. If the trend were to continue, Streep said, "in twenty years [women] will have been eliminated from movies entirely."[aa]

"I'm in my prime," Streep continued. "I want to play the lead, the protagonist who pushes the story forward." She noted that she suppressed a laugh when journalists suggested she should pick different roles: "It's as if they think there's a rainbow of choices. I know what's out there. The range simply isn't there and hasn't been for a long time."[bb]

The speech was a rare show of activism for Streep, and she wasn't entirely comfortable taking such a public stance. "When the day came for the speech I wanted to have all my fingernails [...] pulled out instead of making the speech, because who wants to make this speech? It's only going to hit you in the face," she admitted later. "And then I thought, 'Oh, fuck. Nobody's saying this. Somebody has to say this.'"[cc] This public airing of grievances didn't exactly ingratiate Streep with Hollywood at large. "Her palpable frustration," journalist Rachel Abramowitz wrote, "made the industry see her as petulant rather than heroic, a Cassandra-like figure spouting verities that no one wanted to hear."[dd] It took Hollywood another decade to catch up with Streep, providing her in her fifties and sixties with the meaty protagonist roles that she had lamented not being able to find in her forties. *The Bridges of Madison County* was an early example of the rich lead roles Streep would dine on ten years later as arguably the first middle-aged actress to be taken seriously by Hollywood as a romantic heroine.

Opposite: One of the first
signs of affection between
Francesca and Robert.

Very soon, Robert and
Francesca can't imagine living
without each other.

Following pages: One of the
film's most romantic scenes
takes play in a blues club,
a place where Robert and
Francesca take refuge to
avoid gossip.

their life stories. He talks about having traveled the world as a photographer, having ample adventures (including, he admits, with women), but never building a home. She can't remember how long she's been married and frets that "maybe it's a little dull for you to be talking to some housewife in the middle of nowhere." She acknowledges, almost under her breath, that she had been a schoolteacher for a while but her husband "didn't like me working." She still seems a bit baffled by how she ended up here. "I didn't know anything about Iowa," she says. "I just cared that it was… America. And of course, being with Richard." She brushes off the last phrase, although not so dramatically that it would obviously read as a "tell" in real conversation. Still, Robert is tuned in to her subtext.
"You like living here in Iowa, I guess." He says it as a statement, not a question.
"Mmmm…" Her hesitation says it all. "Yeah."
"Go ahead," he presses. "I won't tell."
"It is quiet. And people are nice, in certain ways," she says. "But…" That "but" is redundant to the distant look on her face.
"But?"
"It's not what I dreamed of. As a girl."
That line recalls Streep's declaration in front of the mirror in *Death Becomes Her*, "I'm a girl!" suggesting that Francesca feels she squandered her one commodity—youthful beauty—on a passionless marriage in which she functions more

as a domestic cog than a person. Robert's effect on Francesca will mimic that of the potion in *Death*—he'll revive her youthful lust for life—and as in Zemeckis's film, that feeling will come with a catch: it's incompatible with life as she knows it.

Francesca relentlessly pursues the feeling, knowing full well it can't last. After their chaste parting that first night, she scrawls a note to him in a frenzy, quoting Yeats's "The Song of Wandering Aengus," a poem about a Celtic god's lifelong search for his loved one. They agree to have dinner together again, but the next day at the town's lone diner he sees the shunning of a woman known to have had an affair with a married man; he is made aware of how those who cross the boundaries of propriety are treated in Iowa. He gives Francesca an out option—which she refuses to take. "Robert," she says, decisively but with fear in her eyes, "I want to come […] don't worry about the rest of it. I'm not."

Why does she do it? Once the relationship is consummated, Francesca tells us via voice-over, "In that moment, everything I knew to be true about myself was gone. I was acting like another woman. And yet I was more myself than ever before." Evidence mounts that the tyranny of small-town domestic life has kept Francesca from becoming "herself" for a long time. One of the most romantic scenes in the film takes place at a roadhouse blues bar, "a place, Robert assured me, no one I knew would see us." In order to escape

Meryl Streep and Clint Eastwood on the set.

Opposite: As he stands in the rain and she sits in her car alone awaiting her husband, for a moment Francesca doesn't know how she feels. However, she decides to sacrifice her love to save her family.

the suffocation of midcentury middle American judgment, they have to delve deep below the surface of the small town, hiding out amid the black community during a time of segregation.

The affair progresses quickly, and soon Robert and Francesca can't imagine living without each other. She packs suitcases the night before her family is due home, but ultimately she tells Robert she can't leave. She can't abandon her family to follow her heart; she knows she'd be sentencing Richard and her kids to a life of misery in their unforgiving community. "Nobody understands," she tells Robert, "that when a woman makes a choice to get married and have kids, in one way her love begins, but in another way, it… stops. You build a life of details, and you just stop and stay steady so that your children can move… but you never think love like this is going to happen to you." She resolves to preserve that extraordinary love by containing it within the four days. And so Robert leaves, and her family returns, "and with them, my life of details."

Once they know the full story, her adult children are so moved by their mother's experience, and the sacrifice of herself that she made for them, that they each take decisive action in their own marriages: Michael embraces his fed-up wife with newfound determination to take her wants and needs seriously, while Carolyn finds the strength to separate from her own drag of a husband and go find herself. So even as the film is saying that Francesca did the right thing by walking away from an affair that made her feel like herself for the first time in her life for the good of the family, it's also suggesting that the appropriate lesson to take from her experience is to enact change in one's own life, that women should be empowered to be who they are.

Finding Francesca

It was by all accounts a blissful production—exactly what Streep needed after her previous grueling jobs. Eastwood and Streep's mutual admiration was so evident that rumors swirled they were repeating the adultery plotline off set, particularly after another actor, Christopher Kroon, told reporters he had seen Eastwood and Streep dancing and holding hands between takes. Asked about the rumors, Streep laughed, while implying the mere accusation was offensive. "It's not even worth responding to. It's like, 'I can't act this?'"[243]

She said she wasn't concerned with the moral implications of the material. "My considerations are more aesthetic ones, like, 'Is this telling the truth?'" Streep said. "To me the people seem real and this could have happened to these people, and if that's true, then that's all it is. It's about two sides of a kind of longing for another life that you don't have."[244] That kind of longing, to feel and experience things outside the realm of possibility

in her own life—including love affairs—was central to her driving motivation to act. "It's a terrible job, you know," she once joked. "I mean, loving all those handsome and fascinating men." Then she laughed. "Come on! It's fun! It's fun to re-create those feelings and not have any of the repercussions. Just think of what lives I've lived vicariously. I've been poisoned by radiation, sent a child to the gas chamber, lost custody of another, lost husbands and lovers. God! If it weren't for the moments when I fell in love, I'd go nuts!"[245]

This wasn't the first time Streep had been the subject of on-set affair rumors—in fact, it was a frequent enough occurrence that all reports had to be taken with a grain of salt. But Streep's performance was still infused with personal experience. In telling the story of a forty-five-year-old woman's journey of self-discovery, the film reflected its female star's feeling that, after years of testing out variations on her identity, fretting about her advancing age in an industry favoring the young, and struggling to balance her desire to take care of her family with her need to find fulfillment outside of the home, she was finally coming into her own. In her forties, she'd later say, "I felt like my clothes finally fit and I didn't have to be anything other than myself."[246]

Eastwood's *Bridges* was perceived by many to be a huge improvement on the novel, in no small part thanks to the changes in perspective that enriched the Francesca character and the masterful minimalism of the two lead performances. Streep's performance is so transparent, so precise in the way it broadcasts internal feeling externally, that it often renders her voice-over redundant. "If anything," wrote John Powers in *Vogue*, "this movie may be too restrained for the mass audience—it lacks the emotional wallop you expect from schmaltz."[247] Ella Taylor was cynical about the movie as a whole ("Thus is your cake—family and fantasy—both had and eaten. Thus is a blockbuster women's picture made"), but she disagreed that the performances were too restrained to deliver feeling. "Have someone wake you for the genuinely wrenching scenes when the lovers part," she wrote. "For the first time in the movie, we get a woman's eye view—Streep at her angry and hurt best—of what it means to lose a lover."[248]

Of course, like the book on which it was based, *Bridges* wasn't made to please critics. "This is the kind of movie that will bring in people who don't usually go to the movies,"[249] predicted Bob Daly of Warner Bros. He was right: the movie grossed $10.8 million in its first weekend, and a full sixty-two percent of the opening weekend crowd was female. Its final take of $71.5 million in the States made *Bridges* Streep's most successful starring vehicle since *Out of Africa*, a figure that would hold up for another decade.

Why did *Bridges* succeed for Streep, allowing her to connect with a mass audience, while so many films across a twenty-year period were greeted with collective shrugs? Perhaps it's as simple as this: it was a role written for a woman of exactly her age, one that allowed her to reveal reserves of naked emotion, and the combination of her age and the seemingly confessional nature of the performance humanized her, brought her down to earth. This much-needed hit gave Streep a vehicle in which to gracefully transition into a new phase as an "older" actress, and it laid the groundwork for her emergence, another ten years later, as a late-blooming baby boomer sex symbol.

After her husband's death, Francesca tries to get in touch with Robert again, but he's nowhere to be found. Some time later, she receives a package from his lawyer. Inside she finds all the souvenirs of their four days together.

8

Miranda Priestly

The Devil Wears Prada (2006)
David Frankel

"I've never run a production company or been in charge of finding material. I've just been available to certain things when I wasn't pregnant."[250]
—Meryl Streep, 2006

A New Millennium

The Gummers moved back to New York City from Connecticut in 2001. By the turn of the century, as Meryl put it, "everybody was graduating from various schools and I did a play in the park"—*The Seagull* in Central Park, her first New York stage production in twenty years—"and had a wonderful time and thought, 'Well, maybe I'll do plays and live in the city.'"[251] They arrived two days before 9/11.

The open wound of the city in fall 2001 matched Streep's state of mind. A lot was going on in her personal life. Her mother died that year, leaving Streep to take over caring for her ill father until his death in 2004. Her return to the New York stage had been made possible by her kids leaving the nest; by 2004, only her youngest, thirteen-year-old Louisa, still lived at home.

Throughout this tumultuous time, Streep's career slowly began to come back to life. *Madison County* had given her a jolt in 1995, but that was an anomaly; throughout the 1990s, her films struggled to connect with the zeitgeist the way they once had. That the Academy still nominated her almost yearly, bestowing credibility on forgettable fare such as *Music of the Heart* (1999) as if on autopilot, added to Streep's public image as a museum piece.

Then, suddenly, in 2002 and 2003 she appeared in three wildly different, high-profile, and rapturously received projects, playing a journalist turned femme fatale in Spike Jonze's *Adaptation* (2002), a middle-aged lesbian in Stephen Daldry's *The Hours* (2002), and several characters in Mike Nichols's miniseries *Angels in America* (2003). These were followed by a deliciously nasty turn as a female senator in Jonathan Demme's 2004 remake of *The Manchurian Candidate*. She also began to come out as a political animal, frequently lashing out at the George W. Bush administration. "What pushed me over the edge?" she asked in 2004. "Name a topic. Everything pushed me over the edge!"[252]

Critic Dennis Lim cited *Adaptation* as a transformative moment for Streep, in that it "basically dramatized the loss of inhibitions that defines this phase of Streep's career."[253] But not everyone was so quick to herald a comeback. In 2006, Karen Hollinger expressed dismay over what she saw as the concluding arc of Streep's stardom: "Her career began progressively with her reshaping underwritten roles to transform negative female portrayals into more positive ones and moved in her middle years into a succession of socially conscious portrayals," Hollinger wrote. "It seems to be concluding rather disappointingly, however, with her typecast in a succession of melodramatic maternal roles of the sort conventionally allotted to older female stars." Hollinger concluded, "It is disheartening to see a career that started so progressively seem to be ending much less so."[254]

And then came *The Devil Wears Prada*.

An Interest in Power

In tracing a naïve college grad's misadventures working for Miranda Priestly, editor of the fictional fashion mag *Runway*, Lauren Weisberger's best-selling novel thinly veiled the author's experience working as an assistant for Anna Wintour, editor in chief of American *Vogue*. Streep was no fan of the book. "I thought it was written out of anger," she said, "and from a point of view that seemed to me very apparent. The girl seemed not to have an understanding of the larger machine to which she had apprenticed. So she was whining about getting coffee for people. If you keep your eyes open [in that situation], you'll learn a lot. But I don't think she was interested."[255]

Luckily, director David Frankel and screenwriter Aline Brosh McKenna did not have a particularly faithful adaptation in mind. "The movie, while noting that she can be sadistic, inconsiderate and manipulative, is unmistakably on Miranda's side," wrote A. O. Scott in the *New York Times*. "How, really, could it be otherwise? In Hollywood, for one thing, an abused assistant is like a Toyota Prius, an indispensable accessory—an entitlement, really—for anyone who even wants to seem powerful."[256]

But the filmmakers weren't after an endorsement of the Hollywood food chain so

Meryl Streep shines as a cold career woman and editor in chief of a fashion magazine in David Frankel's *The Devil Wears Prada* (2006).

Andrea (Anne Hathaway, seated) accepts a position as the assistant to Miranda Priestly (Meryl Streep, standing) even though she aspires to do "real" journalism.

Opposite: Miranda exudes a palpable authority.

Following pages: Young fashion designers face a dreadful trial as they await Miranda's verdict. Here, Miranda and her team are presented with a new collection.

much as an exploration of the power dynamics in a workplace run by women, and that meant adding depth and even empathy to the "devil." The film unfolds through the point of view of Andrea (Anne Hathaway), a fashion-illiterate would-be serious journalist who takes a thankless job as Priestly's assistant in order to pad her résumé. The initially combative, comically sadomasochistic relationship between boss and underling evolves and deepens over the course of the film as both women demonstrate that they can and will do whatever it takes (mistreat a spouse, leapfrog over a friend and colleague) in order to get ahead at work. After both have allowed romantic relationships to die and committed spectacular acts of betrayal in order to protect their own power, Miranda damns Andrea with what she considers praise: "I see a great deal of myself in you." This forces Andrea to question whether or not she really wants to be in this world, if the prize at the end of the road is a life like Miranda has, one of constant work and epic loneliness, with no relationship worth protecting and nothing more important than the acquisition and maintenance of power. "Everybody wants this," Miranda tells Andrea just before putting on her game face to confront a mob of photographers. "Everybody wants to be us." Streep infuses the line with no small amount of irony, implicitly referencing her own conflicted feelings about

celebrity and the peripheral costs and demands of her chosen profession.

Streep herself was fascinated by what she observed as a double standard for professional women, the "special venom" reserved for powerful females like Wintour and Hillary Clinton. "The culture wants to cast them as cold," Streep said, "as if somehow they've lost their maternal bearings, their essential womanhood, to occupy this space. As if they've had to cut off their… whatever it is… to succeed."[257] Plus, "I do think certain things are called 'demands' when they're made by women, and 'he needs his coffee at 10' when they're made by men."[258]

Streep was adamant that while "you can't excuse Miranda's behavior," she could easily feel "if not sympathy, then understanding" of why it was necessary for the character to present herself to the world that way. "There is a certain directness that is necessary as the boss," Streep noted. "The truth is that this is an incredibly high-pressured position; the buck stops with her. If somebody has to get her a cappuccino because she can't run down and stand in line in Starbucks, then suck it up and go get it for her. If she works till 2am to go through the magazine, somebody has to deliver the dry-cleaning. Boo hoo, what a horrible job."[259]

She did not, she insisted, base the character on Wintour. Her cryptic intimations of her actual inspirations were much more interesting.

Top: Meryl Streep discusses
a scene with director
David Frankel.

Bottom: Streep with costume
designer Patricia Field.

Following pages: As she learns
the rules of *Runway*, Andrea
begins to earn Miranda's
respect.

"There were a lot of things I've learned over the years from various bosses I've had—men and women, people of authority with big, big pressures… I had the freedom to imagine how to get my own sweet revenge back on my bosses—and also to express the humanity behind her every external action and to tune into her pain. It was fun to make her as smart as someone who occupies that position has to be."[260]

"Men inspired the character mostly," added director Frankel. "It wasn't the sort of powerful woman you sometimes see out there that was the starting point for Meryl, but really all the men who give up time with their families and put career before everything."[261] Frankel's description could be applied to Dustin Hoffman's character in *Kramer vs. Kramer*. Twenty-seven years later, the struggle to "have it all" was very much a part of the national discourse, and Streep would have the biggest hit of her career by assuming the artfully made-up face of that struggle.

Streep in Charge

Now in her late-fifties, Streep still battled fear and insecurity every time she approached a new part. "Especially now," she said. "I mean, come on; when you have people writing these things, that you're the greatest thing that ever ate scenery, you're dead. You're fucking dead. How can you even presume to begin a new character? It's a killer."[262]

As ever, she papered over trepidation with research. Producer Wendy Finerman gave Streep a binder full of fashion industry statistics. "I thought, 'Oh God, she's going to laugh at me,'" Finerman said. "But instead she said, 'That's fantastic! Do you have any more?'"[263]

Streep was not known for her own fashion savvy; her red carpet looks, which had become increasingly matronly over the years, tended to inspire either catty criticism or shrugs. Fashion was not a world she relished being in, even for the short duration of shooting the movie. "I just found it exhausting," she admitted, "all the attention to details that might as well have been jet engine parts, for all that I cared."[264]

Still, as she often did, Streep took an extraordinarily active role behind the scenes for a performer credited with "just" acting. She essentially functioned as cowriter, acting coach, and even set decorator, helping to select the art for the walls of Miranda's office. She took charge of her character's look, losing seven pounds and working with her long time makeup artist J. Roy Helland to select Miranda's ice-white wig. "I thought, We'll sit down and we'll talk, and Meryl will try on a few things and we'll choose one," said Frankel. "No. Meryl made the decision. She and Roy sent us a photo and said, 'Here's the look.' I said, 'Great.' And the studio were beside themselves and fought it as hard as they could."[265]

Streep did defer to costume designer Patricia Field when it came to couture. "My job was to make Meryl look as absolutely beautiful as I could," Field said. "Not to dictate fashion, but to have people say, 'Wow, Meryl Streep!'"[266]

Now that Streep was the elder stateswoman in a cast of mostly younger performers, she fell into the position of default mentor to the younger actresses on set. Hathaway admired, of all things, Streep's performance in *She-Devil*. "I would have gotten her coffee and done her dry cleaning. It would have been my pleasure. Of course Meryl never took it there." They weren't, Hathaway said, "chummy on set. But never did she make me think it was because of something I did. She told me, 'This is the way I'm playing the character' and not to take it personally. She was always Meryl in rehearsals—warm smile, nicknames, hugs, 'what's going on?' But once she was Miranda, she didn't care about those things, because Miranda didn't care about those things."[267]

Streep envisioned Miranda as a woman who can get whatever she wants without yelling, or even saying a word. According to Frankel, this "came from her experiences with Clint Eastwood and the way he's always in control and ready to go and ahead of everyone in his thinking. He's a strong figure and doesn't need to raise his voice to let anyone know that."[268] In one scene, Andrea's coworker Nigel (Stanley Tucci) explains that Miranda will tell a designer what she thinks of his collection by nodding once (good), nodding twice (very good), or pursing her lips (very bad). When she is then presented a dress and she responds by tilting her head slightly and puckering up, it's like a bomb has gone off in the scene, even though she's barely moved and hasn't made a sound.

As in *Kramer*, in *Prada* Streep's character is discussed more often than she's seen, her presence felt in her absence by the way it impacts the actions and attitudes of the characters given more screen time. And just as she fed her performance with everything "I got from looking in [the other actors'] eyes" on *Sophie*, here she modulated Miranda based on the reactions she was getting from the other performers. "I really, really depend on the other actors for the confirmation of who I think I am," she acknowledged. "And so it's important to me to work with good people that are not worried about how they look." Hathaway's "vulnerability was so palpable that you just couldn't help but eviscerate her," she added. "It's like an animal that offers the neck. She offered her neck, constantly. So I felt like the alpha dog."[269] Hathaway said her costar "would go off book to get my character to where the character should be. She could easily have gotten into her car and gone home when her performance was over. But off-camera Meryl was there trying to make me better. It was humbling that she cared so much about my performance."[270]

In a time of crisis, Miranda opens up to her assistant. It was Streep's idea to have the film reveal the editor-in-chief's vulnerability.

Streep was aggressive in shaping Miranda's arc. "When we first talked about this script, Meryl felt we had pulled our punches in the first act," Frankel admitted. "We'd originally thought Meryl might not want to play someone who was really not likable in some ways, but Meryl said we should make her meaner and, in fact, make her as mean as you can."[271]

Streep also came up with the idea of giving Miranda a scene in which she lets down her guard. Stripped of the armor of makeup, Miranda confides in Andrea that her husband has asked for a divorce. She goes on to give a distinctly Streepy monologue, articulating a mother's concern for what her profession and her notoriety is doing to her daughters, in a manner that's both emotionally naked and dryly cynical. Screenwriter McKenna said the actress wanted to "show that there's a cost. But she's not going to let it get in the way of the things she has to do. She's not just responsible to herself, there's her business and standards to uphold."[272] As Streep explained, it was "the part of the film that makes the whole rest of it worth doing. Without that scene, what is there?"[273]

The Power of a Female Suit

A film about a woman who puts business above all else, *Prada* might not have been made if not for another woman's certainty that it would be good for business.

"*Prada* ran up against some problems about whether it was marketable," Streep noted. "With movie vehicles with women or older women in prominent positions on the one-sheet, it's not ever anything that isn't completely terrifying and shaky, even in the best of circumstances. It's not easy to get these movies financed." Why not? "Movies are people's fantasies. Most of the people who run studios are men. It's not their fantasy, seeing their first wife up there. Their fantasy is somebody more like their second or third wives."[274] Streep claimed that Twentieth Century Fox's top exec, Tom Rothman, had said of *Prada*, "I don't get it. I'm going to say it right now. Go ahead, make the movie, but it's not my thing."[275] Rothman, who Streep had known for three decades, "has two daughters and he has a wife and he has a lot of smart women executives that said, 'Tommy, this will make money. This will make you a lot of money.' And they were right."[276]

One of those women executives was Elizabeth Gabler, who was responsible for bringing a number of "unlikely" female-skewing hits through the pipeline, including *Unfaithful* (2002) and *Walk the Line* (2005). According to Frankel, it was Gabler who finally fixed *Prada*'s third act, in which Andrea tries to warn Miranda about a corporate coup. "Elizabeth stepped in and said, 'You're wasting your time. Miranda would be 100 steps ahead of her. You don't need this girl

to save the day.' Elizabeth's experience as a very successful, professional woman lent a lot to the shaping of the movie."[277]

Streep herself credited the rise of female executives for her career resurgence. "I always thought I'd be washed up at 40. That's the way it is for most leading actresses. I've been lucky. I'm not unaware of the fact that some of my biggest jobs recently have come as a result of women being the head of studios. Amy Pascal was at Sony when Spike Jonze said he wanted me to play the part of Susan Orlean [in *Adaptation*]. I was 52 years old. They could have asked for a 32-year-old. I can't help thinking that if a man had been running that studio they would have asked Cate Blanchett. That was Amy."[278]

Streep's turn in *Prada* could not have been better received. The reviews were not only rapturous, they were philosophical, using this triumph as an excuse to put Streep's career into context, to appraise (and praise) how far she had come. Dennis Lim predicted that if Streep did not win an Oscar for *Prada* (she was nominated, but lost to Helen Mirren's Queen Elizabeth II), it would be because "Streep—in her own iconic, institutional way—is, yes, underrated." He added, "Streep's approach unites the cerebral and the instinctive: She acts at the speed of thought. No other American actor can so deftly and economically convey the contradictory tumult of inner life."[279]

Female critics were particularly impressed by Streep's surprise third act. "When protagonists grow up, they become antagonists," mused Carina Chocano in the *Los Angeles Times*. "Once a beloved star hits unlovable middle age, the thinking goes, audiences love to hate them. [… But Streep] plucks the movie away from its star, and its author, taking full possession of not just the film but of its governing ethos."[280] Ella Taylor hit a similar note: "On the wrong side of 40, when many actresses are squatting in trees, Streep, whose dramatic performances tend toward the overwound and accent heavy, has found her second wind as a comedian," she wrote. ("What a pity, then," she added, "that in the end, *The Devil Wears Prada* flabs out in all the usual ways.")[281]

Without adjusting for inflation, *Prada* was the biggest moneymaker of Streep's career to date. Its opening five-day holiday weekend box office take exceeded its budget. Two thirds of the audience was female, and half was twenty-five or older. By the end of its run, the film had grossed $124 million in the States. Hollywood's businessmen were baffled. Asked *Variety*, "What marketing maven would have predicted that a talky chick flick, produced at a cost of $36 million, would generate an international box office total north of $280 million?"[282]

But Streep was not that surprised. "When you're in high school, you go to the movies that the boy wants to see, and that hasn't changed,"

Andrea becomes indispensable to Miranda, usurping Emily (Emily Blunt), her colleague and friend.

Opposite: "Everyone wants to be us" is the reply Miranda gives when Andrea expresses doubt about her aim in life.

she said. "When they say, 'Oh, but women pick,' women pick because they pick what they think he wants to see. They're not stupid."[283] And as much as *Prada* was easy to dismiss as "a talky chick flick," box office statistics showed that as the film's grosses grew, its audience became increasingly male. Streep could tell the film was having an impact by the response from male fans.

"It was the first time in my life, 30 years of making movies, that a man came up and said, 'I know how you felt. I have a job like that. People don't understand.' First time," she marveled. "Without question, of the heterosexual men that I've spoken to over the years, usually […] they say, you know, 'My favorite thing you've ever done was Linda.' Or Sophie. And they were a particular kind of very feminine, recessive kind of personality. So they fell in love with her, but they didn't feel the story through her body. And it took until *The Devil Wears Prada* to play someone tough, who had to make hard decisions, who was running an organization, and sometimes that takes making tough decisions for a certain kind of man to empathize, feel the story through her."[284]

The theme of the 79th Academy Awards was "Road to the Oscars," and in keeping with that theme, the Academy asked nominees to fill out a brief questionnaire intended to help the awards body "get to know your story and learn more about your personal road to the Oscars." Meryl Streep was nominated that year for her turn as Miranda Priestly in The Devil Wears Prada. *Here are her wonderfully terse, unedited answers to the questionnaire.*

What were your childhood dreams/ambitions?
My childhood ambition was to marry the Prince of Wales and live in a castle and be a translator at the UN. And an Olympic Swimmer and to have curly hair and not have to wear glasses all the time.

What was your first big break?
Marian the librarian in the *Music Man* in high school. You mean after high school? Joe Papp cast me in my first paid job in NY at Lincoln Center in *Trelawny of the "Wells"*. My first film was a small part in *Julia* directed by Fred Zinnemann with Jane Fonda, Vanessa Redgrave, and Jason Robards Jr.

Tell us about your journey on the movie for which you are nominated.
I wanted to know why we vilify women in powerful positions, I wanted to understand the pressures on such a woman.

What was your most amusing moment working on this movie?
I didn't have any.

What was the hardest challenge/obstacle on the movie?
Wearing the shoes.

What was your most memorable moment working on this movie?
Taking off the shoes, highly.

Is there anything else you would like to tell us about yourself?
No.

9

Julia Child

Julie & Julia (2009)
Nora Ephron

"I remember being shocked to find out that Bette Davis was forty or forty-one when she did *All About Eve* and was playing an over-the-hill, done, out of it, you're finished actress. And that she was only fifty when she did *Baby Jane* […] and all those grotesques of witches. You could call them witches. […] And that really has changed, completely changed. Not for everybody, but for me it has changed!"[285]
—Meryl Streep, 2012

In 2008, Streep was feted by the Film Society of Lincoln Center. Watching the clip reel of her greatest hits that night, Streep wished she could send a message to her younger self. "All I could see was this beautiful young woman who was anxious about whether she was too heavy or if her nose was too big. I felt like saying to her, 'Just relax and it will all be ok.'"[286]

The elder Streep seemed to be a living model of that simple piece of advice. By the late 2000s, many of the actresses she had been compared to and/or competitive with for most of her screen career, with the notable exceptions of Diane Keaton and Sigourney Weaver, had all but vanished from mainstream films. Meanwhile, beginning with *The Devil Wears Prada*, Streep would star in four $100-million hits in less than four years. In defiance of the conventional "wisdom" that there was no life for actresses in Hollywood past the age of forty, Streep was emerging, in her late middle age, as not just a box office star but an unlikely sex symbol. In *Prada*, her character was the epitome of glamour; in both *Mamma Mia!* and *It's Complicated*, she played women pursued by multiple suitors, even as they're old enough to have adult children; in *Julie & Julia*, Streep played a not-conventionally-attractive woman in an extraordinarily sexually satisfying marriage. Unusually, and not incidentally, she had to be aged down several decades in order to do so.

Mike Nichols wasn't exaggerating when he said of his frequent collaborator, "She broke the glass ceiling of an older woman being a big star—it has never, never happened before."[287] Jeanine Basinger, a film historian who specializes in the study of female stars, observed that Streep had "matured to a point that very few actresses get to, arriving at the 'Hell, I don't really care anymore' place. She's not afraid to be mean or hated. She's not afraid to be unglamourous. She's more at ease with it. It looks like she's over the career part and just having fun with the roles. That energizes everything she's done." And, Basinger added, there was a direct relationship between Streep's new energy and her late-career emergence as a box office draw. "[Her] presence in a film is an endorsement that says to the ticket buyers that you're not going to be cheated. That is what stardom has come down to—value for your money."[288]

Perhaps the most impressive example of Streep's "value" during this period was *Mamma Mia!*, Phyllida Lloyd's film adaptation of the hit Broadway jukebox musical, whose flimsy love quadrangle narrative ties together the greatest hits of ABBA. Streep was one of the only talented singers cast in a proudly absurd, over-the-top production, which netted dreadful reviews—and grossed over $600 million worldwide, making it Streep's most successful film by many multiples, even adjusting for inflation. It was also a bigger international hit than *Iron Man*, *Quantum of Solace*, and several other male-skewing blockbusters released by studios in 2008.

These numbers meant something: they proved that *Prada* hadn't been a fluke, a spike in Streep's fortunes, the way *Bridges of Madison County* had been in the otherwise tepid previous decade. Something about what Streep was doing was tapping into what audiences—particularly female audiences—wanted to see, at home and around the world. "It's so gratifying," Streep said of *Mamma*'s success, "Because it's [attracting] the audience that nobody really gives a shit about"[289]—"nobody" meaning the male Hollywood marketing geniuses who had been baffled by the success of *Prada*.

Streep was quick to point out that her wave of popularity was "only happening now because there are more women in decision-making positions who are able to greenlight movies."[290] *Mamma*, like *Prada* and other Streep successes of the 2000s, had been supported by a female executive. "Donna Langley was one of our champions at Universal for *Mamma Mia!*," Streep pointed out. "Nobody wanted to make that. The smart guys banked on *Hellboy* [*II: The Golden Army* (2008)] to carry them throughout the year.

Meryl Streep in a very personal performance as the legendary Julia Child in Nora Ephron's *Julie & Julia* (2009).

Opposite: American expatiates in Paris just after the war, Paul and Julia Child (Stanley Tucci and Meryl Streep) make a very loving couple.

Newly settled in Paris, Julia discovers the pleasures of great food.

Following pages: During their first Parisian lunch, Paul encourages Julia to devote herself to her passion for cooking.

The *Mamma Mia!* wagon is pulling all those movies that didn't have any problem getting made. Our budget would have fit in the props budget of *Hellboy*."[291]

And yet in interviews Streep still frequently claimed she had no business acumen at all. "I don't make anything happen," she insisted in 2008. "I sit at home and wait for the phone to ring. Really. Why these opportunities are coming up has less to do with me than all the things I don't understand about how decisions are made here."[292]

That kind of statement reads like faux-naïveté when juxtaposed with others in which Streep demonstrates a clear understanding of both how Hollywood works and how she has been a unique exception to its rules. She seemed to have a very clear understanding of how decisions are made when she noted that "there was for a long time in the movie business a period when a woman was attractive and marriageable or something—not 'marriageable.' *Fuckable* I guess is the word. […] Well, you know what I'm saying—so you substitute something better. […] And then after that, they really didn't know what to do with you until after you were the lioness in winter, right? Until you were seventy, and then it was okay to, you know, *Driving Miss Daisy* or *Trip to Bountiful* or things like that. But that middle period, […] the most vibrant years of a woman's life, arguably, from forty to sixty were completely—nobody

knew what to do with you." How had she been able to become the exception to that rule? "Part of it, I think, has to do with the fact that I wasn't that word that I just said […]. When I was a younger actress, that wasn't the first thing about me."[293]

She also acknowledged that age itself had changed her approach to her work, and to the way she saw herself. "I think you just have to get sick of hearing the accommodation in your approach to things," she said in 2010. "As there begins to be less time ahead of you, you want to be exactly who you are, without making it easier for everyone else."[294]

Streep was certainly aging gracefully, and doing so in a more feminine/feminist culture than had ever before existed in Hollywood. But she was also apparently liberated by her evolving role at home. By 2008, the youngest of the four Gummer children, Louisa, was preparing to go off to college. Streep no longer had a house full of kids to keep her busy (and humble) in her off-hours. She had once said she needed acting as "an outlet" where she could "work out all my murderous thoughts and my weaknesses and my failures and things I don't want to do as a parent or work out on the family."[295] No longer drastically torn between her two "jobs," she no longer needed to pick films to serve as an outlet for who she couldn't be at home.

"I think you're seeing her freedom and her strength and her relief, to have brought four kids

all the way through into hot careers of their own and happy love relationships," observed Mike Nichols. "You still have them invisibly connected to you, but she's free. At last you're not thinking, 'I have to run home,' and things happen out of that freedom that are, if not new, deeper."[296] Streep herself mused that to be suddenly free of day-to-day parenting duties was liberating: "A chasm opens up. You do what you've always promised yourself you would do when you had time to do it."[297]

Wish Fulfillment

Julie & Julia is based on the memoirs of two women of two radically different generations, united by the common theme of self-discovery through cooking. Streep plays Julia Child from her late thirties through her sixties, as she evolves from plucky but purposeless American wife in Paris into cookbook author and finally pioneer of televised cooking instruction. Her story is interwoven into the circa 2002 tale of Julie Powell (Amy Adams), a thirty-year-old drone at a New York City government agency who embarks on a project of cooking her way through Child's mammoth *Mastering the Art of French Cooking* and documenting her progress on a blog (Powell's book *Julie & Julia* was published in 2005). As she cooks, Julie develops an imaginary friendship with Julia, drawing strength from her idol's own struggles, relatively late in life, to come into her own.

The film begins in back lot–perfect Paris, 1949. Julia Child—thirty-seven years old, born in Pasadena, educated formally at Smith College and informally during World War II as a top secret researcher for the Office of Strategic Services—and her US State Department employee husband Paul (Stanley Tucci) have just relocated for his job. The couple's first Parisian meal is a whole fish cooked in, as Julia drools, "buhterrrr." The meal is a revelation. Bored as a housewife, with no children to tend to (a beautifully understated scene implies that this was not a choice), Julia is left with a surplus of free time that must have felt like a comedown after her stint as a secret agent during the war. "What should I do?" she ponders anxiously. "Shouldn't I find something to *do*?" "What is it that you really like to do?" asks Paul, as they dig into yet another decadent meal.

"Eat!" Julia admits grandly and yet self-deprecatingly. She enrolls first in a course for housewives at Le Cordon Bleu, and then crashes a class for more advanced, serious chefs—even after the headmistress tries to intimidate her away, telling her it's all men and very expensive. "You should have seen the way those men looked at me! They thought I was just a frivolous housewife looking for a way to kill time!" Child complains to her husband in the safety of her home after her first day at school. But back in the class with the men, she laughs and jokes and works as hard as she can. The strategy pays off, and soon Julia is invited by two local housewives turned chefs to collaborate on a cooking school and the book that will become *Mastering the Art of French Cooking*. "I've been looking for a career all my life," Julia exclaims, "and I found it!" But her work is not done: for years she struggles to wrangle the cookbook into shape, and to find a publishing house that believes in it, and her. The book was finally published when she was forty-nine, and her public television show *The French Chef* debuted a year later. Her fifties, sixties, and seventies were the most successful times of her life.

Ephron interweaves Julie and Julia's stories, allowing the older woman's adventures to serve as the younger cook's inspirational wish-fulfillment fantasies. Julie and her husband watch old tapes of Julia's TV show and lovingly, goofily imitate her accent later in bed; Julie even starts dressing in Julia's image, donning pearls and vintage housedresses to cook in her tiny apartment kitchen. In her vision, Paul and Julia have an extremely active sex life, their physical desire for one another manifesting in what we're to believe are daily lunchtime romps—their carnal appetites clearly compatible with their appetites for food. Julie's Julia finds that the bigger her personality gets, the more she invests her time and her passion into her cooking career, the more Paul loves her. This is one aspect of the fantasy that won't fly in real life: Julie learns that her own husband will put up with a lot, but he won't become a doormat for the sake of Julie's home-cooked new career.

By structuring the film so that Julia Child's story essentially plays out in the headspace of Julie Powell, Ephron is able to accomplish two things at once. She narrativizes the way memoirs and historical fiction can function as vehicles to drive fantasies as to what the present-day reader might have done in a specific period, or to how they might apply the lessons of the past to their own lives; and, she creates a logical, sturdy crucible for what is perhaps the biggest, most unhinged, and least self-conscious performance of Meryl Streep's career. If the film's energy flags considerably in the Julie sections, in which the biggest drama is a burned bœuf bourguignon, the Julia sections are vibrantly alive and larger-than-life by design. "Nora said, 'You're not really Julia Child, you're Julie's idea of Julia Child,'" Streep said. "So that gave me the freedom to not replicate her so much as to try to find the particular spirit that I kept reading about."[298]

The Height of Performance

There was much that Julia and Meryl didn't have in common. For one thing, Streep had never evinced much interest in or talent for cooking. She never met Child, but they had had a combative correspondence over the issue of fruit and

Top: Streep recreates Child's beloved television show.

Bottom: Julie Powell (Amy Adams) and her husband (Chris Messina) watch Child with delight.

Opposite: In the kitchen, Julia comes into full bloom.

Julia meets two Frenchwomen who are also passionate about food. Here she's seen cooking with Simone Beck (Linda Emond), her longtime collaborator.

vegetable pesticides, which Streep had protested in the 1980s. Streep noted that she had reached out to Child through the nonprofit she had cofounded, Mothers & Others, but the chef "was extremely dismissive," and when Streep accused the American Council for Science and Health, a competing nonprofit with which Child was aligned, of being a front for agrichemical business interests, Child "went nuts. She was mad. She said, 'Well, buh buh buh, this is not a front for industry, we have many reputable scientists on our board,' and blah, blah blah.' You know, saying the same old thing that isn't true."[299]

Streep also pointed out that she and Child had drastically different upbringings. "Women of that time and of that class—we don't like to talk about that in America, but there are classes in America—and she was [...] wealthy, privately educated [...] and they had a way of speaking. I mean, the last person you'd know, who you'd also recognize with that way of speaking, is Katharine Hepburn probably." Streep herself had known girls with that manner of speaking at Vassar: "There was a way of talking that the private school girls had that was different than the way I talked, from New Jersey."[300]

And yet, despite all of this, Streep could relate to Child in that both had broken through plateaus in middle age. "I can never get over the fact that [*Mastering the Art of French Cooking*] was published when she was 50 years old," Streep said.

"So she didn't really become 'Julia Child' until she was 50."[301] Streep acknowledged that she, too, was coming into her own after a tough decade. "What was hard about my 40s was that I had four young children. I had my fourth child at 43, and that was really something. I had some really interesting choices to make because of this new baby and the bigger kids—Louisa is 12 years younger than Henry, who is the oldest. It was about organizing and the least amount of disruption for everybody in the family."[302]

With the internal common ground established, Streep set to work on the physical manifestations of her Julia Child. "I would love to take credit for that performance," said Ephron, "but the truth is that she had read everything about Julia Child, she played the cooking tapes over and over between set-ups, she worked for weeks with Ann Roth to find the character through the costumes, and she even suggested that I cast Stanley Tucci as her husband."[303]

Streep would say that the key to nailing Child's frequently imitated accent was in figuring out and copying how Child breathed. "She has no breath, absolutely none!" Streep marveled. "She always sounded [out of breath]. I feel that way when I'm in the kitchen, don't you?"[304] Streep mimicked this by drawing on what she learned about breathing in her opera lessons forty-five years earlier.

Just five-foot-six, Streep insisted on gaining eight inches of height to play Child accurately.

One of Meryl Streep's most significant personal and professional relationships came to an end in June 2012 with the death of Nora Ephron, the writer of *Silkwood* and *Heartburn* (in which Streep played a barely veiled version of Ephron herself) and the screenwriter-director of *Julie & Julia*. "I got the news very late," Streep said. "I started to clean and make dinner. There are female activities that make things OK—'and now the next minute you'll do this and everyone has to eat—and that's how you get through the day.'" She added, "That's what recipes were to Nora."[ee] As a friend and a collaborator, Streep had witnessed Ephron's transformation from journalist to screenwriter to auteur. "She had a put-together spine of tensile strength," Streep marveled. "She would wave her arms airily in front of her, like a girl, gracefully. You were manipulated into doing what she wanted. It's very hard to hide the sweat." Ephron had a notorious gift for entertaining, reflected in Streep's likening of an Ephron set to a dinner party: "For Nora, working on the set was like having some people over and if there's some time here's what we'll do."[ff] In 2004, at Streep's American Film Institute Life Achievement gala, Ephron brought down the house by joking that "the true stretch" of Streep's storied career had been "playing me." Ephron deadpanned, "She plays all of us better than we play ourselves, although it's a little depressing knowing that if you went to audition to play yourself, you would lose out to her. Some days, when I'm having a hard day, I call up Meryl, and she'll come and she'll step in for me. She's so good, people don't really notice."[gg] Eight years later, Ephron included Streep on a wish list of desired speakers for her memorial, which made the actress, as she told the assembled mourners, feel "so privileged and so pissed off and so honored and so inept all at the same time that I can't help thinking that this is exactly what she intended."[hh] Imagining her own funeral, Ephron had once said, "I want everyone to be a basket case."[ii] One last time, Streep stepped in and gave her exactly what she wanted.

Meryl Streep and director
Nora Ephron on the set
of *Julie & Julia*.

"I didn't know how she was going to do it," Ephron said. "For me, she didn't have to be six-foot-two. But for her, she had to be six-foot-two. For me, she needed to be Meryl Streep playing Julia Child. But for Meryl, everything was about her height."[305] In the end, the effect was accomplished via sky-high heels, risers, and camera angles to help her tower over Tucci. Streep grew out as well as up: "I gained 15 pounds," she admitted. "I'm still trying to lose it. It was worth it."[306]

One of the reasons why Streep was so intent on modeling Child's unusual height was that she saw how it had impacted the cook's life. "[She] was outsized in her world," Streep noted. "And that was a handicap in the days when the main reason to go to Smith College was to get a husband."[307] Marked as an outsider in a community through no fault of her own, it took Child years to find her place, both romantically and professionally. Streep knew how that felt—after all, she had never been a typical Hollywood actress—and was excited about being able to portray a screen romance that shattered the conventional, superficial Hollywood mold.

"When you're playing romantic characters, a great part of my attention has to be that I look really attractive," Streep mused. "Obviously you can't play a romantic character if she's not really pretty. What's liberating about these characters is that there's this huge throbbing love between two people who don't look like our normal package of lovers. It made it more real and intimate because somehow those concerns were thrown away. If you've been married for a long time you love without looking. I don't assess how my husband looks every single day and think, is he cute enough or whatever? And I sure hope he doesn't do it to me!"[308]

Ephron described the marriage between Paul and Julia as "a wild uncritical love."[309] At the same time, she wanted to make a movie about a happy marriage extending through time, continuing through good times and bad. "You just do not see any movies about marriage. You see movies about people who fall in love [...] and then the movie ends when they say, 'Will you marry me?' That thing, that quotidian thing about marriage that we all love so much, the 'what's for dinner?' of it, that to me was something that I was really happy with when it was over."[310]

"Haute Cuisine Disguised as Comfort Food"

Julia opened opposite *G.I. Joe: The Rise of Cobra* (2009), a clear counterprogramming gambit that paid off. *Julia* grossed $20 million domestically its first weekend, attracting an audience that was two-thirds older and female. It was Streep's third comic hit in four summers. Though she was not Hollywood's highest paid actress or, technically, a more profitable presence than younger stars like Angelina Jolie and Jennifer Aniston, no other actress, according to the *Hollywood Reporter*, "approaches Streep's ability to trigger a green light for a nongenre, mainstream Hollywood movie."[311]

Streep's newfound commercial clout hadn't done anything to cool her critical acclaim. In fact, the chances she was taking in the roles she chose, the new looseness apparent in her approach, resulted in some of the best reviews of her career. It seemed that she could do no wrong; she was even praised where she had previously been attacked, for failing to fully submerge herself in the role. As A. O. Scott wrote in the *New York Times*, "Ms. Streep's Julia Child is never anything other than a performance, a fusion of two strong personalities rather than the absorption by one into another. You never forget that you are watching Meryl Streep inhabiting a version of Julia Child, and instead of distracting you from the truth of Julia, this awareness is what enables you to understand her."[312]

Streep's presence in films that, generically, might otherwise be brushed off as femme fluff, seemed to be enough to prepare critics to take the movies themselves seriously. "Like Nora Ephron's captivating film," wrote Carrie Rickey in the *Philadelphia Inquirer*, "Streep's performance is haute cuisine disguised as comfort food, a complex preparation yielding effects both broadly entertaining and subtly moving."[313] Added Dana Stevens of *Slate*, "The relationship at the heart of this movie—between a female mentor and pupil who never meet but who share a common passion and a drive to reinvent themselves—is one you don't often see depicted in the movies. *Julie & Julia* makes deboning a duck a feminist act and cooking a great meal a creative triumph."[314] Streep, who had been sneaking feminine and feminist perspectives into films for thirty years, was now getting credit for it—for what was, ironically, only the second film of her career, after *Mamma Mia!*, to be written, directed and shepherded at a studio by women.

Streep's finger-on-the-pulse moment was cemented by her ability to turn a subtly feminist film about an unconventional (and not conventionally sexy) woman's sensual triumphs into a critical and commercial hit. This defied every rule about Hollywood ageism—something that her middle-aged female collaborators were quick to point out. Amy Pascal, head of *Julia*'s distributor, Sony, credited Streep with eradicating the industry's conventional wisdom about older women. Ephron agreed: "There's never quite been a career like this," declared *Julia*'s screenwriter/director. "It's hard to think of any woman who not only kept working after a certain age but didn't have to do character roles. This thing of hers, where she is as hot as Will Smith, it's hilarious, and it is such amazing news for those of us who write movies that she's perfect for."

Ephron added, "I'm sitting here knowing that I got a picture made because she wanted to do it. How lucky is that for all of us who like to make movies about women?"[315]

Streep was nominated for an Oscar for *Julia*, but she barely made an effort to campaign for herself and was easily trumped for the best actress prize by Sandra Bullock. Streep had a consolation prize in the form of *It's Complicated*—a glossy fantasy sex farce starring Streep as a self-sufficiently wealthy, divorced sixty-year-old who suddenly finds herself in a love triangle—which opened in December 2009 and ultimately made over $200 million worldwide. The film's success served as a barometer for Streep for how much had changed over the course of her time in movies. "In the period of *Silkwood*, [a movie] could never have been made, with a 60-year-old actress deciding between her ex-husband and another man. With a 40-year-old actress it would never have been made."[316] She added, "It's incredible—I'm 60, and I'm playing the romantic lead in romantic comedies!" Streep exclaimed. "Bette Davis is rolling over in her grave."[317]

In *Julia*, Streep dramatized a decade and a half in the life of a woman whose own career was unprecedented, who faced obstacles and failed, who was told she'd never succeed at what she wanted to do, but who kept butting her head against different parts of the wall until finally she found a place where she could break through. Child's arc to triumph was not so different from the path Streep herself had been on since the late eighties. With *She-Devil*, *Death Becomes Her*, and the other films of that era, Streep had committed herself to a series of comedies about women that reflected her own experience but peddled their critique too stridently for the taste of most audiences. She absorbed lessons from that string of failures, and then she tried again, coming back with a string of comedies not just about women but patently designed for them. *Prada*, *Mamma*, *Julia*, and *It's Complicated* were all packaged blatantly as "chick flicks," which meant that some would dismiss them out of hand as silly or frivolous or cartoonish—but it also meant that they could pass as "mere" entertainment, allowing them to smuggle their socially nutritive content in the wrapping of mass-commercial product. And yes, all of these films did have social value: they depicted types of women who exist in the real world, who, if not for Streep, would likely not be seen on-screen.

Put simply, Streep's first wave of female comedies commented on the opportunities available for women in commercial culture; her second string changed that culture.

"She's always been the most highly decorated actress of our time, but there's real artistic freedom that comes with enormous box office success," noted *Prada* director David Frankel. "For years, she played opposite all these male movie stars who made fortunes, and now suddenly at age 60, she cashed in, not because she went out and did action movies, but she scored doing movies she loves and embraced. That power is liberating."[318]

Streep had made over half a dozen films in three years—the hardest she had worked in her life. In 2009, Streep's youngest child graduated high school and left home for college. Streep's three films released that year (*Julia*, *Complicated* and *Fantastic Mr. Fox* [voice only]) had a combined domestic gross of over $227 million, making Streep second only to her forty-five-year-old Oscar rival Bullock as both the most bankable *and* most honored actress in Hollywood. She wasn't taking any of it for granted. As Streep put it, "I'm very fucking grateful to be alive."[319]

The bond the Childs share is apparent even in this scene where Paul takes pictures of Julia's culinary achievements.

10

Margaret Thatcher

The Iron Lady (2011)
Phyllida Lloyd

"Next to climate, the changing status of women in the last hundred years is the most destabilizing thing that's happened on Earth. It's precipitated so many seismic changes and reactions in cultures. I think you can lay all the fundamentalism that's been rearing its ugly head in the world at the feet of that change."[320]
—Meryl Streep, 2007

In 2002, Meryl Streep earned her thirteenth Oscar nomination, for *Adaptation*, thus breaking the record for most acting nominations in history, jointly held by one of her idols (Katharine Hepburn) and one of her sometime costars (Jack Nicholson). By 2010, when Streep pulled far ahead of all record book competitors in receiving her sixteenth nomination, for *Julie & Julia*, she was widely considered the most revered actress of all time. At the same time, for all her acclaim, the fact that she hadn't actually won an Academy Award in the nearly twenty years since *Sophie's Choice* helped to feed, as Dennis Lim wrote in the *Los Angeles Times*, "a sense in which Streep's greatness is taken for granted. Lost in the routine affirmations of her sacrosanct status is the uncanny probability that she is getting better—and more surprising—with age."[321]

A reliable given of the Academy Awards is that when a performer is passed over for one or more deserving performances, the voting body will remunerate them by awarding a lesser-loved role, because it is now their "turn." Streep's losing streak-breaking best actress win in 2012, for starring as Margaret Thatcher in *The Iron Lady*, could be considered belated canonization of her entire late-career renaissance. That Oscar was about more than individual performances. Her middle-aged lesbian in *The Hours*, her corporate queen in *The Devil Wears Prada*, her sexually active seniors in *Mamma Mia!* and *It's Complicated*—these were all types of women who were not routinely seen on-screen, living lives that had not previously been the concern of Hollywood films. Throughout the first decade of the twenty-first century, Streep had not only resuscitated her own career at an uncommonly advanced age, she had proven to be the exception to the deeply ingrained truism, articulated in *The First Wives Club* (1996), that "there are three roles in Hollywood for women: babe, district attorney, and *Driving Miss Daisy*." Sure, it was the role that most resembled Miss Daisy that actually earned Streep the Oscar—but Rome wasn't built in a day, and neither will Hollywood be so quickly transformed.

Perhaps the most compelling evidence that Academy voters meant for Streep's *Iron Lady* Oscar to cover other recent roles is the simple fact that the movie itself—much like other films showcasing performances awarded because the performer was overdue—is simply not very good. In fact, those who praised Streep's performance as Thatcher rarely condoned the film on the whole. Directed by Streep's *Mamma Mia!* helmer Phyllida Lloyd, *Lady* takes a page from their previous collaboration, giving the jukebox musical-cum–romantic comedy treatment to the life story of the most powerful woman in Western history. The film fully sympathizes with its title character, painting her opponents as irrational, violent, stodgy, and/or misogynist. It even avoids the opportunity to say anything at all intelligent or insightful about the conundrums faced by a woman of Thatcher's stature. Streep's performance, a Swiss-watch-perfect show of technique validating the criticisms she attracted earlier in her career, is all surface, a weirdly soulless facsimile. The East Coast liberal Streep admitted she and the unflinchingly conservative Thatcher were as far apart politically as could be imagined, and yet, it's clear that Streep understood something about Thatcher that another actress might not have. She was able to pull off an exemplary, if frustratingly superficial, animation of a character by relying on shared experience. *The Iron Lady* is not a satisfying biography of Margaret Thatcher; it's much more interesting as a thickly veiled autobiography of Meryl Streep.

How Meryl Became Maggie

Phyllida Lloyd acknowledged that merely making a movie that sought to get inside the head of the controversial Thatcher "was one provocation; casting somebody outside of England in so much of an English role was another."[322] Though Streep was not the obvious choice for the part, the director eventually decided that there was a symmetry that made the casting perfect. "Meryl's being an outsider is a mirror of Thatcher being an

The role of Margaret Thatcher in Phyllida Lloyd's *The Iron Lady* (2011) earned Meryl Streep the third Oscar of her career.

Moving back and forth between past and present, the film reveals how much the elderly Margaret Thatcher (Meryl Streep) is haunted by her dead husband, Denis (Jim Broadbent).

outsider in the Tory party," Lloyd noted, adding, "therefore you have Meryl coming in and having to work harder than one of our great English actresses would have had to work. Having to do more preparation, stay up later, just work, work, work to be able to stay up there on the tightrope."[323]

As per usual, Streep prepared by drowning herself in research. She attended a session of parliament on January 20, 2011, watching a debate between David Cameron and Labour leader Ed Miliband. She spoke to people close to Thatcher, who, she said, "were very forthcoming about both her strengths and her, well, not so much her weaknesses, as her character defects, perhaps. She did have a cruelty to her, and I did learn how she paid a price for it."[324] She listened to ample recordings of Thatcher speaking, both as a young woman and later, after she learned to control and deepen her tone. Streep found it "fun" to imitate Thatcher's recorded voice: "She had a very particular way of emphasizing points, and making her point. That had to do with bringing out a word that you didn't normally think was the most important word in the sentence. And she also had a thing of taking a breath and starting quietly, making her point in a way that you don't know that this point is going to be made through several examples and there will not be a break in the speaking voice at any point, and if you think you're going to interrupt, you're really not going to have the opportunity because she's just got capacity. It's really stunning."[325]

Again, the cardiovascular control that Streep learned as a teenage opera student came in handy here. "I did need a lot of breath. I needed a lot more breath than I have, after all my expensive drama school training. I couldn't keep up with her."[326]

"I think that voice lessons really just bring out a voice that you already possess," noted Streep, who, of course, had ample experience with such coaching.[327] Still, the effect in the film—as Margaret's voice evolves from Alexandra Roach's adolescent timbre to Streep's shrill bellow as the novice parliamentarian, to her calmer but still cartoonish intonations as Thatcher in her prime— is not that the character is becoming more herself, but that her voice is becoming more affected as she loses touch with reality.

Streep wanted the makeup and prosthetics she wore in order to transform into an aged Thatcher to serve a purpose, "changing the outside to get at something inside." J. Roy Helland, Streep's makeup artist since *Sophie's Choice*, collaborated with British prosthetics designer Mark Coulier. Months before shooting began, Streep, Helland, and Coulier began working together, creating casts of Streep's face and testing different solutions. "And I would say, inevitably, 'Less, less, less, less,'" Streep noted.

She added, "It's not about the audience, it's all about fooling the other actors into believing that you are who you say you are. Because that's hard, when you walk on set with this big makeup job—it makes it hard for them. And I take my entire performance from them. So if they don't look at me and hate me appropriately, or love me the way they're supposed to, find an old face but see the young one underneath—which is Jim Broadbent's task—then I'm lost. I don't have anything to go on. Because I can read that immediately."[328]

A Makeover Movie

In the first scenes of *Lady*, Streep is heavily aged-up to play Thatcher in the film's present day, as a doddering dowager unfit for twenty-first-century London. Thatcher, buying milk at a corner store, is wrapped in a headscarf and not recognized as the former female leader of the free world; the actress who plays her, acting mostly via beautifully understated reaction, is likewise completely unrecognizable.

This relatively subtle, almost-realism doesn't last long. The film essentially takes place in the elder Thatcher's dementia-stricken mind, flashing back and forth between the ex–prime minister's vivid, exaggerated, and whitewashed memories of her rise to the top, and her gray and morbid retirement life, in which much time is devoted to remembering how to do basic household tasks. Time and space collapse in her mind, clouding her view of the real world. Literally haunted by the ghost of her late husband Denis (Jim Broadbent), present-day Maggie has but one struggle: to pack up and get rid of the contents of Denis's closet. As Streep summed it up, "It's three days in an old lady's life, when she's decided to upend her life and move her husband's things out of her world."[329]

Lloyd gives Thatcher's life and misadventures the same music-montage heavy, kaleidoscopic and time-flattening treatment that worked for the lark of *Mamma Mia!*. In the context of a historical fiction, this formal strategy cheapens Thatcher's experiences even as it's glorifying them. The backbone to the narrative is not the march of time in a rapidly evolving world, but Thatcher's personal transformation, which hits all the beats of a classic woman's melodrama. She arcs from plucky working-class college girl to would-be small-time politico turned housewife who warns her proposing beloved that she won't be contained by a kitchen ("One's life must matter, Denis, beyond all the cooking, the cleaning, and the children—I cannot die washing up a tea cup!") to ball-busting MP and PM literally waltzing through history with a string of world leaders as partners. She then falls, suddenly, into the role of tragically delusional, barely functional widow.

Throughout, the flashpoints of Thatcher's life are shown to be the moments when her essential self meets resistance, and she either stands her ground or acquiesces in the name of strategy.

Young Margaret Roberts (Alexandra Roach) suffers her first electoral defeat.

Opposite: To reach the highest political posts, Margaret Thatcher is handed over to two consultants in charge of making her over so she matches the expectations of the British electorate.

She learns repeatedly that the way she presents herself as a woman will have to be molded into new, user-friendly forms if she wants to get ahead in a man's world. At a dinner party, the young Margaret (played by Alexandra Roach) expounds on her economic beliefs in gendered terms ("A man might call it fiscal responsibility; a woman might call it good housekeeping!") while both male and female guests titter in derision. Later, after her first political failure, Denis proposes marriage as a career proposition, telling her it will help the men in charge take her seriously, legitimizing her as a woman in power by softening her, so that she's not perceived as a shrew.

But Mrs. Thatcher, now played by Streep, can't win either way: she's treated as a harridan in Parliament ("The right honorable lady doth screech too much!" complains a colleague) and is an absentee at home. Her rise to the highest level of English politics is presented, literally, as a makeover, complete with catty comments on her personal fashion made by men. "You look and sound like a privileged, conservative wife," declares one of two male consultants brought in to make Maggie electable. She's given new clothes, new hair, and a new voice, because "people don't want to be harangued by a woman, hectored. Persuaded, yes." Ambitious Margaret eagerly follows the advice of the worldly men, although she insists she's holding on to at least a small aspect of her essence: "Gentleman, I am in your

hands. But the pearls," she says, gripping the strand around her neck, "are absolutely nonnegotiable."

Rather than play as though Lloyd and writer Abi Morgan borrowed tropes from chick flicks in order to animate the potentially dull life of a female politician, *The Iron Lady* feels like it's exploiting political events to add substance to a chick flick. Its central question—is it possible for a woman to become the best in a male-dominated field without sacrificing at home and/or losing her mind?—is essentially the same as the dilemma faced by the women of *The Devil Wears Prada*. Thatcher is thus brought down to earth, her problems shown to be qualitatively the same as any working woman's— a disingenuous notion at best.

Indeed, *Lady*'s depiction of the mundane sexism faced by strong women in the workplace is often quite a bit more facile than *Prada*'s. Thatcher's all-male cabinet is shown trying to get through to her about her insensitive policies while she's having an evening gown tailored to her body, with one side of her bra exposed in plain sight. When she protests that she's not out of touch, because she knows how much butter costs, the men giggle and whisper under their breath. Later, on the eve of the Falklands War, when her foreign policy credentials are questioned, the camera moves in as Streep intones, "With all due respect, sir, I have done battle every day of my life, and many men have underestimated me before."

Delivering a speech before Parliament, Thatcher shows great political resolve while being booed and laughed at by the opposition.

Opposite: Streep is unrecognizable as Rabbi Chemelwitz in Mike Nichols's *Angels in America* (2003).

Streep gives the line a pomposity that plays as unexamined and unearned; it's impossible to imagine a female boss speaking this way to colleagues in real life. It gets worse, more forced in its "irony": she then stands up and asks the US secretary of state how he takes his tea.

Vocally, Streep's impersonation of Thatcher is astonishingly exact; physically, she's able to animate excessive old-age makeup with an authentic-feeling heaviness befitting Thatcher's confusion. But it doesn't feel like there's a living person at the center of the performance, and maybe more than anything, this owes to a script that treats Thatcher's experience of knee-jerk misogyny as a punctuating punch line.

Unlikely Kindred Spirits

Streep's Thatcher has much in common with Streep's Julia Child in that both required extreme physical and vocal transformations to serve an imitation of real, famous people—and both seemed to overshoot the mark of reality, capturing an exaggerated version of the woman that reflected their image within culture as being larger-than-life.

Streep acknowledged that there was a vocal similarity between the two characters, with the crucial difference being that "she's so alive, Julia Child. And Margaret is so […] *designed*."[330] And it's in that aspect of design that Meryl and Margaret are unlikely kindred spirits: as we've seen, Streep, starting at a very young age, was hyperaware that her freedom of movement as a woman had much to do with the way she presented herself—to men and to her peers. Both very savvily designed public personas for themselves in order to maximize their credibility, because they knew that as powerful women in their fields, they were under much more powerful microscopes than their male counterparts.

And as Julia reflected Streep's own later-in-life blooming, *The Iron Lady* dealt with issues close to Streep's heart while mirroring aspects of her own experiences as an ambitious woman. "The themes in the film […] have interested me for awhile. And you never see those subjects covered in films normally," she said. Those themes included "Women and power and diminishment of power and loss of power. And reconciliation with your life when you come to a point when you've lived most of it and it's behind you."[331]

These connections came despite the fact that Streep couldn't align herself with Thatcher ideologically. "My friends and I are all, well, let's say we play for the other team," Streep admitted. Still, she was "secretly quite delighted that a woman had been elected head of the United Kingdom—and by the conservative party, no less. Back then, there weren't women in government. It was very rare indeed, and so we were all thinking, 'If this can happen in gender-biased,

Meryl Streep has often said that she wouldn't be able to do what she does if it weren't for the talents of her supporting actors and crew. In 2012, when she was awarded an Honorary Golden Bear at the Berlin Film Festival, Streep used to occasion to salute a previously unsung hero of her career, her hair and makeup artist J. Roy Helland. "Roy has worked with me since my first play in New York more than 35 years ago," Streep said. "The first film we did together was *Sophie's Choice*. And he has designed every woman— and one man, in *Angels in America*—that I've played ever since then."[jj]

Streep has described Helland as her closest collaborator when it comes to the process of character creation. "He's always, always with me," she has said, "and he understands the job and changing the outside to get at something inside."[kk] Helland, who previously worked with Liv Ullmann and on the sets of films such as *Working Girl* (1988) and *Bugsy* (1991), won an Emmy for designing Streep's transformations in *Angels in America* but had never been recognized by the Academy for his work. Then came *The Iron Lady*. When his name was announced as the winner of best makeup (alongside Mark Coulier) on Oscar night in 2012, Streep got so excited that she jumped up and the belt broke off of her golden gown. In his brief acceptance speech, the makeup artist was quick to credit his canvas: "Thanks, Meryl, for keeping me employed for the last 37 years," Helland said. "Your brilliance makes my work look good no matter what."[ll]

As for their relationship, Streep summed it up thusly: "A person puts their hands on your face for a couple of hours. You really have to like them. Certainly, you have to be not annoyed by them. But he's particularly gifted, and we have a good collaboration. In other words, he does what I say. Like Margaret Thatcher, I'm very patient provided I get my own way in the end."[mm]

This page and opposite: Margaret Thatcher triumphs as leader of the Conservative Party, eventually becoming the first female Prime Minister.

Following pages: After the positive outcome of the Falklands War, Margaret Thatcher defends her stance on sending British troops to respond to Argentine aggression.

homophobic England, it can happen in America, too.' We really thought we'd get a woman President within five years. Of course, we're still waiting for that one."[332]

Streep noted that, in the US, anti-Thatcherism "was blended with anti-Reaganism, but there was a special venom reserved for her, I felt, because she was a woman."[333] (Note that Streep used the same phrase, "special venom," when talking about her attraction to Miranda Priestly.) Streep takes over the portrayal of Thatcher at age forty-nine, when she became the leader of the Conservative Party, the first woman to attain that political office in Britain. In 1979, when she was elected prime minister, it was a shock. Britain had not exactly been fully remade by the feminist movement, making a female leader of the nation controversial among members of her generation; at the same time, young activist women couldn't hold up Maggie as one of their own. "I owe nothing to women's lib," Thatcher herself said in 1982. "She would have been kicking and screaming the entire way to the feminist altar," said Streep, "but she was a feminist, whether she likes it or not."[334] Streep's comment suggests that Thatcher was uncomfortable being branded as a feminist, at least in part because of the perception that it could limit her actual progress as a woman striving for equal footing with men—a phenomenon that Streep was familiar with.

Ever drawn to disagreeable women, those who dare to challenge gender dichotomies by reaching for opportunities and experiences commonly reserved for men, Streep also admired and could relate to Thatcher's resolve. "She wasn't saying to everyone, 'Well, how do you all feel about this? What do you think I should do about it?' No, she took a stance and stood by it—that was how she approached her work and, in my own life, that's how I approach mine. Every character I have ever played I have thrown myself into and become very defensive about them and protective of them, and that is what she and I have in common."[335]

In another interview, Streep expounded on her empathy for Thatcher. "With any character I play, where she is me is where I meet her. It's very easy to set people at arm's length and judge them. Yes, you can judge the policies and the actions and the shortcomings—but to live inside that body is another thing entirely. And it's humbling on a certain level and infuriating, just like it is to live in your own body. Because you recognize your own failings, and I have no doubt she recognized hers."[336]

Writing History

Months before the movie was released, British tabloids began to unveil reports that friends of Thatcher had seen the film and were "revolted" by the "inaccuracies" of its depiction. The *Daily Mail* even published an infographic breaking

down "Five Ways the Film Gets It Wrong." The first on this list was the film's suggestion that when Thatcher announced she was pursuing the Tory Party leadership, her husband angrily suggested she was putting "ambition before me and the children." In real life, according to the paper, "Sir Denis told his wife, 'I will back you all the way, love.'"[337] The movie's version is more dramatic—and more faithful to the stock tropes of career woman cinema.

Streep didn't give credence to such criticisms. "The most transgressive thing we have done in this film is to imagine Margaret Thatcher—who is characterized in many quarters as a monster, a person who has trampled all that was great in Britain—to imagine her as human. That's the biggest transgression in our film is to imagine her 360 [degrees], and to me that's just really interesting that that's a crime. But it's the artist's job to go there."[338]

Despite Streep's defense, most reviews did not harp on this transgression; most simply suggested the film was unsatisfying as a political or historical drama. The *Los Angeles Times* published two essays arguing that the film was a letdown. For film critic Betsy Sharkey, despite "Streep's uncanny ability to disappear inside her characters," the film completely lacked "insight into the intrigues of her very long political life."[339] Theater critic Charles McNulty, who wrote the movie off as "a montage of photo ops strung together with Wikipedia factoids," rained on the parade of Streep's twenty-first-century resurgence, noting that "the overriding effect" of roles as seemingly disparate as Streep's in *Prada*, *Julia*, *Mamma Mia!*, and *Iron Lady* "is one of elaborate imposture." He added, "her characterizations are so well calculated that they call attention to their own artistry. The dancer is always distinguishable from the dance."[340]

Of course, the Academy loves that kind of performance—the "elaborate" transformation that constantly reminds the viewer of a movie star's unusual labor. Years earlier, Streep had explained that there was some truth to the canard, "It's an honor just to be nominated": "That's because actors vote for the acting nominees; the general membership votes for the winners. So winning may not be considered as *informed* an honor as a nomination. I don't think people really understand that."[341]

The Iron Lady was distributed in the United States by master Oscar campaigner Harvey Weinstein, and Streep seemed to exert an unusual amount of effort promoting herself, appearing on every talk show and even on the cover of *Vogue* (making her the oldest woman ever to do so). Still, up until the very end, the smart money was on best actress going to Streep's *Doubt* (2008) costar Viola Davis, nominated for *The Help* (2011). Come Oscar night, when Streep's name was announced

as the winner, the seventeen-time nominee, fourteen-time loser threw her head back and laughed.

"It was like [I was] a kid again," Streep marveled backstage. "I was a kid when I won this, like, 30 years ago." Implicitly referring to best actress competitors Rooney Mara and Michelle Williams, she added, "Two of the nominees were not even conceived."[342]

At the podium, Streep said, "I really understand that I'll never be up here again." Chalk this up to Streep's tendency for downplaying her achievements via extreme modesty, the "nothing-to-see-here" misdirection that she uses to distance herself from the spotlight, to allow her work to breathe. Given her track record and the fact that she shows no sign of slowing down (in 2013 she'll turn sixty-four and is scheduled to appear in two movies, John Wells's adaptation of the Tracy Letts play *August: Osage County* and *The Homesman*, directed by and costarring Tommy Lee Jones), it wouldn't be wise to bet against her.

Previous pages: Streep admired Thatcher's refusal to compromise her beliefs.

Streep with director Phyllida Lloyd.

Conclusion

Meryl Streep had noted she had been drawn to the role of Margaret Thatcher in part because she was interested in "reconciliation with your life when you come to a point when you've lived most of it and it's behind you."[343] She was clearly thinking about her own legacy. In late 2011, Streep used the platform of the *Iron Lady* press tour to reveal that she had personally donated $1 million to a drive to raise $400 million in private funds for the construction of a new National Women's History Museum in Washington, DC. She was hoping, she said, to literally help rewrite history. "History until the 20th century was written by one member of the human family, and it wasn't the mother. It was dad. That's who wrote history and…what was important? Movements of armies, sovereignty of nations, all sorts of things. But women were there all along, and they have incredible stories that we don't know anything about."[344]

Thanks to Streep, there are dozens of incredible female stories that we do know about. The experiences of women touched by war. The struggle for independence in the feminist backlash era. Businesswomen, bored housewives, late-blooming gurus and lovers and activists. The Prime Minister of England. Aging actresses.

For years it seemed like Streep struggled to balance work and life, her personal passions, and her instinct for self-preservation through savvy self-promotion. Earlier in her career, Streep might have shied away from her similarities to Margaret Thatcher when talking about making the movie; she might have insisted that, as a full-time mom and part-time movie star, she didn't know a thing about "women and power and diminishment of power and loss of power." Instead, at age sixty-two, she aligned herself with the powerful historical figure she had just played, and in using the spotlight on the movie to shine attention on the National Women's History museum, embraced her own role as a woman who could make things happen. Maybe even change history.

Following pages: Meryl Streep plays a lesbian editor in Stephen Daldry's *The Hours* (2002).

Chronology

1949
Born Mary Louise Streep on June 22, in Summit, New Jersey.

1961
After a triumph at a school recital, begins taking opera singing lessons from Estelle Liebling.

1967
Enrolls in Vassar College, where her lead performance in *Miss Julie* cements her as the campus star.

1971
Graduates from Vassar. Takes a year off and performs with the touring company Green Mountain Guild.

1972–1975
Attends graduate school at the Yale School of Drama, where her classmates include playwright Christopher Durang and Sigourney Weaver.

1975
Moves to New York, where Joseph Papp casts her in productions of *Trelawny of the "Wells"* and *Measure for Measure*. She goes on to appear in nine additional plays in New York in the next five years.
Meets and starts dating John Cazale.

1977
Makes her Broadway debut, in *Happy End*.
Lands her first film role, a supporting part in *Julia*.
Cast as "Linda" in *The Deer Hunter*, alongside Robert De Niro and real-life boyfriend, Cazale.
Shoots TV miniseries *Holocaust* in Austria.

1978
Nurses cancer-stricken John Cazale, who dies in March.
Shoots *The Seduction of Joe Tynan*, *Manhattan*, and *Kramer vs. Kramer*.
Wins Emmy Award for *Holocaust*.
Marries sculptor Don Gummer.

1979
Nominated for her first Oscar for *The Deer Hunter*.
Son, Henry Wolfe Gummer, is born.

1980
Wins first Oscar, for best supporting actress as Joanna Kramer in *Kramer vs. Kramer*, on her second nomination.

1981
Plays a dual role in *The French Lieutenant's Woman*; nominated for third Oscar, for best actress.
Stars in musical off-Broadway production of *Alice in Concert*, her last New York stage appearance for twenty years.

1982
Stars as "Sophie" in *Sophie's Choice*, for which she wins her first best actress Oscar.

1983
Daughter Mary Willa "Mamie" Gummer is born.
Stars as Karen Silkwood in *Silkwood*; nominated for fifth Oscar, for best actress.

1984
Reteams with Robert De Niro to play an adulterous couple in *Falling in Love*.

1985
Stars as Karen Blixen in *Out of Africa*; nominated for sixth Oscar, for best actress.
Leaves New York City, moves with her family to Connecticut.
Named Hollywood's biggest female box office draw by *Boxoffice* magazine.

1986
Daughter Grace Jane Gummer is born.
Stars as "Rachel Samstat," an autobiographical character written by Nora Ephron, in *Heartburn*, her second film directed by Mike Nichols.

1987
Plays an alcoholic vagrant opposite Jack Nicholson in *Ironweed*; nominated for seventh Oscar, for best actress.

1988
Stars as Lindy Chamberlain in *A Cry in the Dark*; nominated for eighth Oscar, for best actress.

1989
Takes her first comedic starring role, opposite Roseanne Barr in *She-Devil*.
Turns forty.

1990
Streep and family buy a house in Los Angeles.
Plays "Suzanne Vale," a character based on screenwriter Carrie Fisher, in *Postcards from the Edge*, her third film directed by Mike Nichols; nominated for ninth Oscar, for best actress.
Delivers keynote speech to the first Screen Actors Guild National Women's Conference, denouncing sexism within the film industry.

1991
Daughter Louisa Jacobson Gummer is born.
Stars opposite Albert Brooks in *Defending Your Life*.
Amid falling out with Mike Nichols, leaves longtime agent Sam Cohn at ICM for Bryan Lourd at CAA.

1992
Stars as aging actress "Madeline Ashton" in *Death Becomes Her*.

1994
The Gummers move back to Connecticut.
Takes her first action role in *The River Wild*.

1995
Stars opposite Clint Eastwood in *The Bridges of Madison County*; receives tenth Oscar nomination, for best actress.

1998
Stars in *One True Thing*; receives eleventh Oscar nomination, for best actress.

1999
Learns to play violin for her role in *Music of the Heart*; receives twelfth Oscar nomination, for best actress.

2001
Appears in her first New York

play in twenty years,
a production of *The Seagull*
in Central Park.
The Gummers move back
to New York City from
Connecticut.

2002

Takes key supporting roles
in *The Hours* and *Adaptation*;
receives thirteenth Oscar
nomination, for best
supporting actress, for
the latter.

2003

Plays multiple roles in Mike
Nichols's TV miniseries
Angels in America; receives
second Emmy Award.

2004

Costars in Jonathan Demme's
remake of *The Manchurian
Candidate*.
Receives American Film
Institute Life Achievement
Award.

2006

Stars in Tony Kushner's
update of *Mother Courage
and Her Children* at New
York's Public Theater.
Plays the villainous Miranda
Priestly in *The Devil Wears
Prada*; receives fourteenth
Oscar nomination, for best
actress.

2008

Sings, dances, and chooses
between three suitors as star
of *Mamma Mia!*
Honored by the Film Society
of Lincoln Center.
Included in the inaugural class
of the New Jersey Hall of
Fame, alongside Albert
Einstein, Frank Sinatra, and
Toni Morrison.
Celebrates thirty-year
wedding anniversary with
Don Gummer.
Appears in *Theater of War*, a
documentary chronicling the
production of *Mother Courage*
that offers a rare glimpse of
Streep's process.
Stars in John Patrick Shanley's
Doubt; receives fifteenth Oscar
nomination, for best actress.

2009

Stars in *It's Complicated* and
Julie & Julia, earning her
sixteenth Oscar nomination,
for best actress, for the latter.

2010

While appearing in the
documentary series *Faces
of America with Henry Louis
Gates, Jr.*, discovers that she
and Mike Nichols are distant
cousins.

2011

Stars as Margaret Thatcher
in *The Iron Lady*; wins her
third Oscar, for best actress,
on her seventeenth
nomination.
Becomes the public face of
the effort to establish a
National Women's History
Museum on the Mall in
Washington, DC, donating
$1 million to the cause.

2012

Awarded Honorary Golden
Bear at the Berlin Film
Festival.
Films *August: Osage County*,
based on the Tracy Letts play.

Page 174:
Top, left: Streep in Jerry
Schatzberg's *The Seduction
of Joe Tynan* (1979).

Top, right: Streep in
Karel Reisz's *The French
Lieutenant's Woman* (1981).

Bottom, left: Streep in Hector
Babenco's *Ironweed* (1987).

Bottom, right: Streep in
Fred Schepisi's *A Cry in the
Dark* (1988).

Opposite:
Top, left: Streep in Robert
Altman's *A Prairie Home
Companion* (2006).

Top, right: Streep in Robert
Redford's *Lions for Lambs*
(2007).

Bottom, left: Streep in John
Patrick Shanley's *Doubt*
(2008).

Bottom, right: Streep
in Nancy Meyers's
It's Complicated (2009).

Following page:
Top, left: Robert Benton's
Still of the Night (1982).

Top, right: Fred Schepisi's
Plenty (1985).

Bottom, left: Clint Eastwood's
*The Bridges of Madison
County* (1995).

Bottom, right: Phyllida Lloyd's
The Iron Lady (2011).

If looks could kill...

STILL OF THE NIGHT

Meryl Streep
Plenty

CLINT EASTWOOD   MERYL STREEP

THE BRIDGES OF
MADISON
COUNTY

WARNER BROS. Presents
An AMBLIN/MALPASO Production CLINT EASTWOOD MERYL STREEP "THE BRIDGES OF MADISON COUNTY" Music by LENNIE NIEHAUS
Edited by JOEL COX Production designed by JEANNINE OPPEWALL Director of photography JACK N. GREEN a.s.c. Screenplay by RICHARD LaGRAVENESE
Based on the novel by ROBERT JAMES WALLER Produced by CLINT EASTWOOD and KATHLEEN KENNEDY Directed by CLINT EASTWOOD

NEVER COMPROMISE.

MERYL STREEP
The
IRON LADY

Filmography

1977

The Deadliest Season (TV movie)
Directed by Robert Markowitz *Screenplay* Ernest Kinoy, based on a story by Tom King and Ernest Kinoy *Cinematography* Alan Metzger *Original Music* Dick Hyman *Film Editing* Stephen A. Rotter *Produced by* Robert Berger. With Meryl Streep (Sharon Miller), Michael Moriarty (Gerry Miller), Kevin Conway (George Graff), Sully Boyar (Tom Feeney), Jill Eikenberry (Carol Eskanazi), Walter McGinn (District Attorney Horace Meade).

Julia
Directed by Fred Zinnemann *Screenplay* Alvin Sargent, based on a story by Lillian Hellman *Cinematography* Douglas Slocombe *Original Music* Georges Delerue *Film Editing* Marcel Durham and Walter Murch *Produced by* Richard Roth. With Meryl Streep (Anne Marie), Jane Fonda (Lillian Hellman), Vanessa Redgrave (Julia), Jason Robards (Dashiell Hammett), Maximilian Schell (Johann), Hal Holbrook (Alan Campbell), Rosemary Murphy (Dottie Campbell).

Great Performances (TV series)
"Secret Service" (Season 5, Episode 7, January 12, 1977)
Directed by Peter Levin *Screenplay* William Gillette, based on his play *Produced by* Ken Campbell. With Meryl Streep (Edith Varney), John Lithgow (Capt. Thorne), Mary Beth Hurt (Caroline Mitford), Frederick Coffin (Lt. Maxwell), Lenny Baker (Henry Dumont), Charles Kimbrough (Benton Arrelsford).

1978

Holocaust (TV miniseries)
"The Gathering Darkness" (Part I, April 16, 1978)
"The Road to Babi Yar" (Part II, April 17, 1978)
"The Saving Remnant" (Part IV, April 19, 1978)
Directed by Marvin J. Chomsky *Screenplay* Gerald Green *Produced by* Robert Berger. With Meryl Streep (Inga Helms Weiss), James Woods (Karl Weiss), Michael Moriarty (Erik Dorf), Deborah Norton (Marta Dorf), Fritz Weaver (Josef Weiss), Rosemary Harris (Berta Palitz Weiss), Joseph Bottoms (Rudi Weiss), Tovah Feldshuh (Helena Slomova), Sam Wanamaker (Moses Weiss), Ian Holm (Heinrich Himmler), David Warner (Reinhard Heydrich).

The Deer Hunter
Directed by Michael Cimino *Screenplay* Deric Washburn, based on a story by Michael Cimino, Deric Washburn, Louis Garfinkle, and Quinn K. Redeker *Cinematography* Vilmos Zsigmond *Original Music* Stanley Myers *Film Editing* Peter Zinner *Produced by* Michael Cimino, Michael Deeley, John Peverall, and Barry Spikings. With Meryl Streep (Linda), Robert De Niro (Michael), John Cazale (Stan), John Savage (Steven), Christopher Walken (Nick), George Dzundza (John).

1979

Manhattan
Directed by Woody Allen *Screenplay* Woody Allen and Marshall Brickman *Cinematography* Gordon Willis *Set Decoration* Robert Drumheller *Film Editing* Susan E. Morse *Produced by* Charles H. Joffe and Jack Rollins. With Meryl Streep (Jill), Woody Allen (Isaac Davis), Diane Keaton (Mary Wilke), Michael Murphy (Yale), Mariel Hemingway (Tracy), Anne Byrne Hoffman (Emily).

Great Performances (TV series)
"Uncommon Women... and Others" (Season 6, Episode 10, June 20, 1979)
Directed by Merrily Mossman and Steve Robman *Screenplay* Wendy Wasserstein, based on her play *Produced by* Phyllis Geller. With Meryl Streep (Leilah), Swoosie Kurtz (Rita Altabel), Jill Eikenberry (Kate Quin), Ann McDonough (Samantha Stewart), Ellen Parker (Muffet DiNicola), Alma Cuervo (Holly Kaplan).

The Seduction of Joe Tynan
Directed by Jerry Schatzberg *Screenplay* Alan Alda *Cinematography* Adam Holender *Set Decoration* Alan Hicks *Original Music* Bill Conti *Film Editing* Evan A. Lottman *Produced by* Martin Bregman. With Meryl Streep (Karen Traynor), Alan Alda (Joe Tynan), Barbara Harris (Ellie Tynan), Rip Torn (Senator Kittner), Melvyn Douglas (Senator Birney), Charles Kimbrough (Francis), Carrie Nye (Aldena Kittner).

Kramer vs. Kramer
Directed by Robert Benton *Screenplay* Robert Benton, based on a novel by Avery Corman *Cinematography* Nestor Almendros *Set Decoration* Alan Hicks *Original Music* Erma E. Levin *Film Editing* Gerald B. Greenberg *Produced by* Stanley R. Jaffe. With Meryl Streep (Joanna Kramer), Dustin Hoffman (Ted Kramer), Jane Alexander (Margaret Phelps), Justin Henry (Billy Kramer), Howard Duff (John Shaunessy), George Coe (Jim O'Connor).

1981

Kiss Me, Petruchio (TV documentary)
Directed by Christopher Dixon. With Meryl Streep (Katherine), Raul Julia (Petruchio), John Bottoms (Gremio), Joel Brooks (Grumio), Max Gulak (Baptista).

The French Lieutenant's Woman
Directed by Karel Reisz *Screenplay* Harold Pinter, based on a novel by John Fowles *Cinematography* Freddie Francis *Set Decoration* Ann Mollo *Original Music* Carl Davis *Film Editing* John Bloom *Produced by* Leon Clore. With Meryl Streep (Sarah/Anna), Jeremy Irons (Charles Henry Smithson/Mike),

Hilton McRae (Sam), Emily Morgan (Mary), Charlotte Mitchell (Mrs. Tranter), Lynsey Baxter (Ernestina).

1982
Alice at the Palace (TV movie)
Directed by Emile Ardolino *Screenplay* Elizabeth Swados, based on novels by Lewis Carroll *Produced by* Joseph Papp. With Meryl Streep (Alice), Debbie Allen (Red Queen), Betty Aberlin (Alice's sister), Richard Cox (Mad Hatter), Rodney Hudson (Cheshire Cat/unicorn).

Still of the Night
Directed by Robert Benton *Screenplay* Robert Benton, based on a story by Robert Benton and David Newman *Cinematography* Nestor Almendros *Set Decoration* Steven J. Jordan *Original Music* John Kander *Film Editing* Gerald G. Greenberg and Bill Pankow *Produced by* Arlene Donovan. With Meryl Streep (Brooke Reynolds), Roy Scheider (Dr. Sam Rice), Jessica Tandy (Grace Rice), Joe Grifasi (Joseph Vitucci), Sara Botsford (Gail Phillips).

Sophie's Choice
Directed by Alan J. Pakula *Screenplay* Alan J. Pakula, based on a novel by William Styron *Cinematography* Nestor Almendros *Set Decoration* Carol Joffe *Original Music* Marvin Hamlisch *Film Editing* Evan A. Lottman *Produced by* Keith Barish and Alan J. Pakula. With Meryl Streep (Sophie), Kevin Kline (Nathan), Peter MacNicol (Stingo), Rita Karin (Yetta).

1983
Silkwood
Directed by Mike Nichols *Screenplay* Nora Ephron and Alice Arlen *Cinematography* Miroslav Ondricek *Set Decoration* Derek R. Hill and Dennis W. Peeples *Original Music* Georges Delerue *Film Editing* Sam O'Steen

Produced by Michael Hausman and Mike Nichols. With Meryl Streep (Karen Silkwood), Kurt Russell (Drew Stephens), Cher (Dolly Pelliker), Craig T. Nelson (Winston), Diana Scarwid (Angela), Ron Silver (Paul Stone).

1984
Falling in Love
Directed by Ulu Grosbard *Screenplay* Michael Cristofer *Cinematography* Peter Suschitzky *Set Decoration* Steven J. Jordan *Original Music* Dave Grusin *Film Editing* Michael Kahn *Produced by* Marvin Worth. With Meryl Streep (Molly Gilmore), Robert De Niro (Frank Raftis), Harvey Keitel (Ed Lasky), Jane Kaczmarek (Ann Raftis), George Martin (John Trainer), David Clennon (Brian Gilmore), Dianne Wiest (Isabelle).

1985
Plenty
Directed by Fred Schepisi *Screenplay* David Hare, based on his play *Cinematography* Ian Baker *Original Music* Bruce Smeaton *Film Editing* Peter Honess *Produced by* Joseph Papp and Edward R. Pressman. With Meryl Streep (Susan Traherne), Charles Dance (Raymond Brock), Tracey Ullman (Alice Park), John Gielgud (Sir Leonard Darwin), Sting (Mick), Ian McKellen (Sir Andrew Charleson), Sam Neill (Lazar).

Out of Africa
Directed by Sydney Pollack *Screenplay* Kurt Luedtke, based on books by Karen Blixen (a.k.a. Isak Dinesen), Judith Thurman, and Errol Trzebinski *Cinematography* David Watkin *Set Decoration* Josie MacAvin *Original Music* John Barry *Film Editing* Pembroke J. Herring, Sheldon Kahn, Fredric Steinkamp, and William Steinkamp *Produced by* Sydney Pollack. With Meryl Streep (Karen), Robert

Redford (Denys), Klaus Maria Brandauer (Bror), Michael Kitchen (Berkeley), Malick Bowens (Farah), Joseph Thiaka (Kamante).

1986
Heartburn
Directed by Mike Nichols *Screenplay* Nora Ephron, based on her novel *Cinematography* Nestor Almendros *Set Decoration* Susan Bode *Original Music* Carly Simon *Film Editing* Sam O'Steen *Produced by* Robert Greenhut and Mike Nichols. With Meryl Streep (Rachel Samstat), Jack Nicholson (Mark Forman), Jeff Daniels (Richard), Maureen Stapleton (Vera), Stockard Channing (Julie Siegel), Richard Masur (Arthur Siegel), Catherine O'Hara (Betty), Steven Hill (Harry Samstat).

1987
Ironweed
Directed by Hector Babenco *Screenplay* William Kennedy, based on his novel *Cinematography* Lauro Escorel *Set Decoration* Leslie A. Pope *Original Music* John Morris *Film Editing* Anne Goursaud *Produced by* Keith Barish and Marcia Nasatir. With Meryl Streep (Helen Archer), Jack Nicholson (Francis Phelan), Carroll Baker (Annie Phelan), Michael O'Keefe (Billy Phelan), Diane Venora (Margaret "Peg" Phelan), Fred Gwynne (Oscar Reo), Margaret Whitton (Katrina Dougherty), Tom Waits (Rudy).

1988
A Cry in the Dark
Directed by Fred Schepisi *Screenplay* Robert Caswell and Fred Schepisi, based on a non-fiction book by John Bryson *Cinematography* Ian Baker *Original Music* Bruce Smeaton *Film Editing* Jill Bilcock *Produced by* Verity

Lambert. With Meryl Streep (Lindy Chamberlain), Sam Neill (Michael Chamberlain), Bruce Myles (Barker), Nick Tate (Charlwood), Charles Tingwell (Justice Muirhead), Neil Fitzpatrick (Phillips).

1989
She-Devil
Directed by Susan Seidelman *Screenplay* Barry Strugatz and Mark R. Burns, based on a novel by Fay Weldon *Cinematography* Oliver Stapleton *Set Decoration* George DeTitta Jr. *Original Music* Howard Shore *Film Editing* Craig McKay *Produced by* Jonathan Brett and Susan Seidelman. With Meryl Streep (Mary Fisher), Roseanne Barr (Ruth Patchett), Ed Begley Jr. (Bob), Linda Hunt (Hooper), Sylvia Miles (Mrs. Fisher).

1990
Postcards from the Edge
Directed by Mike Nichols *Screenplay* Carrie Fisher, based on her novel *Cinematography* Michael Ballhaus *Set Decoration* Chris Butler *Original Music* Carly Simon *Film Editing* Sam O'Steen *Produced by* John Calley and Mike Nichols. With Meryl Streep (Suzanne Vale), Shirley MacLaine (Doris Mann), Dennis Quaid (Jack Faulkner), Gene Hackman (Lowell Kolchek), Richard Dreyfuss (Dr. Frankenthal), Rob Reiner (Joe Pierce).

1991
Defending Your Life
Directed by Albert Brooks *Screenplay* Albert Brooks *Cinematography* Allen Daviau *Set Decoration* Linda DeScenna *Original Music* Michael Gore *Film Editing* David Finfer *Produced by* Michael Grillo. With Meryl Streep (Julia), Albert Brooks (Daniel Miller), Rip Torn (Bob Diamond), Lee Grant (Lena Foster), Buck Henry (Dick Stanley).

1992

Death Becomes Her

Directed by Robert Zemeckis *Screenplay* Martin Donovan and David Koepp *Cinematography* Dean Cundey *Set Decoration* Jackie Carr *Original Music* Alan Silvestri *Film Editing* Arthur Schmidt *Produced by* Steve Starkey and Robert Zemeckis. With Meryl Streep (Madeline Ashton), Bruce Willis (Dr. Ernest Menville), Goldie Hawn (Helen Sharp), Isabella Rossellini (Lisle von Rhuman), Ian Ogilvy (Chagall).

1993

The House of the Spirits

Directed by Bille August *Screenplay* Bille August, based on a novel by Isabel Allende *Cinematography* Jörgen Persson *Set Decoration* Søren Gam *Original Music* Hans Zimmer *Film Editing* Janus Billeskov Jansen *Produced by* Bernd Eichinger. With Meryl Streep (Clara del Valle Trueba), Glenn Close (Férula Trueba), Jeremy Irons (Esteban Trueba), Winona Ryder (Blanca Trueba), Antonio Banderas (Pedro Tercero Garcia), Vanessa Redgrave (Nívea del Valle), Vincent Gallo (Esteban García).

1994

The River Wild

Directed by Curtis Hanson *Screenplay* Denis O'Neill *Cinematography* Robert Elswit *Set Decoration* Rick Gentz *Original Music* Jerry Goldsmith *Film Editing* David Brenner and Joe Hutshing *Produced by* David Foster and Lawrence Turman. With Meryl Streep (Gail Hartman), Kevin Bacon (Wade), David Strathairn (Tom Hartman), Joseph Mazzello (Roarke Hartman), John C. Reilly (Terry), Benjamin Bratt (Ranger Johnny).

1995

The Bridges of Madison County

Directed by Clint Eastwood *Screenplay* Richard LaGravenese, based on a novel by Robert James Waller *Cinematography* Jack N. Green *Set Decoration* Jay Hart *Original Music* Lennie Niehaus *Film Editing* Joel Cox *Produced by* Clint Eastwood and Kathleen Kennedy. With Meryl Streep (Francesca Johnson), Clint Eastwood (Robert Kincaid), Annie Corley (Carolyn Johnson), Victor Slezak (Michael Johnson), Jim Haynie (Richard Johnson), Sarah Kathryn Schmitt (Young Carolyn), Christopher Kroon (Young Michael).

1996

Before and After

Directed by Barbet Schroeder *Screenplay* Ted Tally, based on a novel by Rosellen Brown *Cinematography* Luciano Tovoli *Set Decoration* Gretchen Rau *Original Music* Howard Shore *Film Editing* Lee Percy *Produced by* Susan Hoffman and Barbet Schroeder. With Meryl Streep (Dr. Carolyn Ryan), Liam Neeson (Ben Ryan), Edward Furlong (Jacob Ryan), Julia Weldon (Judith Ryan), Alfred Molina (Panos Demeris), Daniel von Bargen (Fran Conklin).

Marvin's Room

Directed by Jerry Zaks *Screenplay* Scott McPherson, based on his play *Cinematography* Piotr Sobocinski *Set Decoration* Tracey A. Doyle *Original Music* Rachel Portman *Film Editing* Jim Clark *Produced by* Robert De Niro, Jane Rosenthal, and Scott Rudin. With Meryl Streep (Lee), Leonardo DiCaprio (Hank), Diane Keaton (Bessie), Robert De Niro (Dr. Wally), Hume Cronyn (Marvin).

1997

...First Do No Harm (TV movie)

Directed by Jim Abrahams *Screenplay* Ann Beckett *Cinematography* Pierre Letarte *Set Decoration* Wayne Jacques *Original Music* Hummie Mann *Film Editing* Terry Stokes *Produced by* Jim Abrahams. With Meryl Streep (Lori Reimuller), Fred Ward (Dave Reimuller), Seth Adkins (Robbie Reimuller), Allison Janney (Dr. Melanie Abbasac), Margo Martindale (Marjean).

1998

Dancing at Lughnasa

Directed by Pat O'Connor *Screenplay* Frank McGuinness, based on a play by Brian Friel *Cinematography* Kenneth MacMillan *Original Music* Bill Whelan *Film Editing* Humphrey Dixon *Produced by* Noel Pearson. With Meryl Streep (Kate "Kit" Mundy), Michael Gambon (Father Jack Mundy), Catherine McCormack (Christina "Chrissy" Mundy), Sophie Thompson (Rose "Rosie" Mundy).

One True Thing

Directed by Carl Franklin *Screenplay* Karen Croner, based on a novel by Anna Quindlen *Cinematography* Declan Quinn *Set Decoration* Elaine O'Donnell and Leslie A. Pope *Original Music* Cliff Eidelman *Film Editing* Carole Kravetz Aykanian *Produced by* Jesse Beaton and Harry J. Ufland. With Meryl Streep (Kate Gulden), Renée Zellweger (Ellen Gulden), William Hurt (George Gulden), Tom Everett Scott (Brian Gulden), Lauren Graham (Jules), Nicky Katt (Jordan Belzer).

1999

Music of the Heart

Directed by Wes Craven *Screenplay* Pamela Gray *Cinematography* Peter Deming *Set Decoration* George DeTitta Jr. *Original Music* Mason Daring *Film Editing* Gregg Featherman and Patrick Lussier *Produced by* Susan Kaplan, Marianne Maddalena, Allan Miller, and Walter Scheuer. With Meryl Streep (Roberta Guaspari), Cloris Leachman (Assunta Guaspari), Aidan Quinn (Brian Turner), Angela Bassett (Janet Williams), Gloria Estefan (Isabel Vasquez), Jane Leeves (Dorothea von Haeften), Henry Dinhofer (Lexi at 5), Michael Angarano (Nick at 7).

2002

Adaptation

Directed by Spike Jonze *Screenplay* Charlie Kaufman, based on a novel by Susan Orlean *Cinematography* Lance Acord *Set Decoration* Gene Serdena *Original Music* Carter Burwell *Film Editing* Eric Zumbrunnen *Produced by* Jonathan Demme, Vincent Landay, and Edward Saxon. With Meryl Streep (Susan Orlean/Susan's mother), Nicolas Cage (Charlie Kaufman/Donald Kaufman), Tilda Swinton (Valerie Thomas), Chris Cooper (John Laroche), Jay Tavare (Matthew Osceola), Cara Seymour (Amelia Kavan).

The Hours

Directed by Stephen Daldry *Screenplay* David Hare, based on a novel by Michael Cunningham *Cinematography* Seamus McGarvey *Set Decoration* Philippa Hart *Original Music* Philip Glass *Film Editing* Peter Boyle *Produced by* Robert Fox and Scott Rudin. With Meryl Streep (Clarissa Vaughan), Julianne Moore (Laura Brown), Nicole Kidman (Virginia Woolf), Stephen Dillane (Leonard Woolf), John C. Reilly (Dan Brown), Ed Harris (Richard Brown), Allison Janney (Sally Lester).

2003

Freedom: A History of Us (TV miniseries)
"Independence" (Season 1, Episode 1, 2003)
Directed by Philip Kunhardt III, Peter W. Kunhardt and Nancy Steiner *Produced by* Philip Kunhardt III and Peter W. Kunhardt, Christopher Reeve, Nancy Steiner, and Brian Brunius. With Meryl Streep (Abigail Adams), Philip Bosco (Samuel Adams), Michael Caine (William Pitt), Richard Gere (Patrick Henry), Tom Hanks (Paul Revere), Anthony Hopkins (George Washington), Jeremy Irons (Thomas Paine), Kevin Kline (Thomas Jefferson).

Freedom: A History of Us (TV miniseries)
"Liberty for All?" (Season 1, Episode 3, 2003)
Directed by Philip Kunhardt III, Peter W. Kunhardt, and Nancy Steiner *Produced by* Philip Kunhardt III and Peter W. Kunhardt, Christopher Reeve, Nancy Steiner, and Brian Brunius. With Meryl Streep (Mary Easty), Kevin Kline (Thomas Jefferson), Jeremy Irons (King James I), Ralph Fiennes (William Bradford), Anthony Hopkins (John Winthrop), Michael Caine (The Rev. John Cotton), John Lithgow (Roger Williams).

Freedom: A History of Us (TV miniseries)
"Yearning to Breathe Free" (Season 1, Episode 10, 2003)
Directed by Philip Kunhardt III, Peter W. Kunhardt, and Nancy Steiner *Produced by* Philip Kunhardt III and Peter W. Kunhardt, Christopher Reeve, Nancy Steiner, and Brian Brunius. With Meryl Streep (Mother Jones), Philip Bosco (Edouard de Laboulaye), Stanley Tucci (Frederick Bartholdi), Harry Connick Jr. (Joseph Pulitzer), Matthew McConaughey (Mark Twain),

Blythe Danner (Emma Lazarus), Jane Alexander (Jane Addams).

Freedom: A History of Us (TV miniseries)
"Democracy and Struggles" (Season 1, Episode 13, 2003)
Directed by Philip Kunhardt III, Peter W. Kunhardt, and Nancy Steiner *Produced by* Philip Kunhardt III and Peter W. Kunhardt, Christopher Reeve, Nancy Steiner, and Brian Brunius. With Meryl Streep (Margaret Chase Smith), Charles S. Dutton (Negro Student), Morgan Freeman (Thurgood Marshall), Paul Newman (Justice Earl Warren).

Angels in America (TV miniseries)
Directed by Mike Nichols *Screenplay* Tony Kushner *Cinematography* Stephen Goldblatt *Set Decoration* George DeTitta Jr. *Original Music* Thomas Newman *Film Editing* John Bloom and Antonia Van Drimmelen *Produced by* Celia D. Costas. With Meryl Streep (Hannah Pitt/Ethel Rosenberg/The Rabbi), Al Pacino (Roy Cohn), Justin Kirk (Prior Walter), Ben Shenkman (Louis Ironson), Emma Thompson (Nurse Emily), Patrick Wilson (Joe Pitt), Mary-Louise Parker (Harper Pitt), Jeffrey Wright (Belize).

2004

The Manchurian Candidate
Directed by Jonathan Demme *Screenplay* Daniel Pyne and Dean Georgaris, based on a novel by Richard Condon and on a screenplay by George Axelrod (1962) *Cinematography* Tak Fujimoto *Set Decoration* Leslie E. Rollins *Original Music* Rachel Portman *Film Editing* Carol Littleton and Craig McKay *Produced by* Jonathan Demme, Ilona Herzberg, Scott Rudin, and Tina Sinatra. With Meryl

Streep (Eleanor Shaw), Denzel Washington (Ben Marco), Liev Schreiber (Raymond Shaw), Jon Voight (Senator Thomas Jordan), Kimberly Elise (Rosie), Jeffrey Wright (Al Melvin).

Lemony Snicket's A Series of Unfortunate Events
Directed by Brad Silberling *Screenplay* Robert Gordon, based on the novels by Daniel Handler *Cinematography* Emmanuel Lubezki *Set Decoration* Cheryl Carasik *Original Music* Thomas Newman *Film Editing* Michael Kahn *Produced by* Laurie MacDonald, Walter F. Parkes, and Jim Van Wyck. With Meryl Streep (Aunt Josephine), Jim Carrey (Count Olaf), Liam Aiken (Klaus Baudelaire), Emily Browning (Violet Baudelaire), Kara and Shelby Hoffman (Sunny), Billy Connolly (Uncle Monty).

2005

Prime
Directed by Ben Younger *Screenplay* Ben Younger *Cinematography* William Rexer *Set Decoration* Carol Silverman *Original Music* Ryan Shore *Film Editing* Kristina Boden *Produced by* Jennifer Todd and Suzanne Todd. With Meryl Streep (Lisa Metzger), Uma Thurman (Rafi Gardet), Bryan Greenberg (David Bloomberg), Jon Abrahams (Morris).

2006

A Prairie Home Companion
Directed by Robert Altman *Screenplay* Garrison Keillor, based on a story by Garrison Keillor and Ken LaZebnik *Cinematography* Edward Lachman *Set Decoration* Tora Peterson *Film Editing* Jacob Craycroft *Produced by* Robert Altman, Wren Arthur, Joshua Astrachan, Tony Judge, and David Levy. With Meryl Streep (Yolanda Johnson), Lily Tomlin (Rhonda Johnson), Lindsay

Lohan (Lola Johnson), Woody Harrelson (Dusty), Tommy Lee Jones (The Axeman), Garrison Keillor (G.K., himself), Kevin Kline (Guy Noir).

The Music of Regret (Short musical)
Directed by Laurie Simmons *Screenplay* Laurie Simmons and Matthew Weinstein *Cinematography* Edward Lachman *Original Music* Michael Rohatyn *Film Editing* Laura Israel *Produced by* Jeanne Greenberg Rohatyn and Donald Rosenfeld. With Meryl Streep (The Woman), Adam Guettel (The Man), and the Alven Ailey II dancers.

The Devil Wears Prada
Directed by David Frankel *Screenplay* Aline Brosh McKenna, based on a novel by Lauren Weisberger *Cinematography* Florian Ballhaus *Set Decoration* Lydia Marks *Original Music* Theodore Shapiro *Film Editing* Mark Livolsi *Produced by* Wendy Finerman. With Meryl Streep (Miranda Priestly), Anne Hathaway (Andy Sachs), Emily Blunt (Emily), Stanley Tucci (Nigel), Simon Baker (Christian Thompson), Adrian Grenier (Nate).

2007

Dark Matter
Directed by Shi-Zheng Chen *Screenplay* Billy Shebar, based on a story by Shi-Zheng Chen and Billy Shebar *Cinematography* Oliver Bokelberg *Set Decoration* Les Boothe *Original Music* Van Dyke Parks *Film Editing* Michael Berenbaum and Pam Wise *Produced by* Andrea Miller, Mary Salter, and Janet Yang. With Meryl Streep (Joanna Silver), Liu Ye (Liu Xing), Aidan Quinn (Jacob Reiser), Joe Grifasi (Professor Colby), Blair Brown (Hildy), Lei Tsao (Zhang Ming), Jing Shan (Wang Ying).

Evening
Directed by Lajos Koltai
Screenplay Susan Minot and Michael Cunningham, based on a story by Susan Minot *Cinematography* Gyula Pados *Set Decoration* Catherine Davis *Original Music* Jan A. P. Kaczmarek *Film Editing* Allyson C. Johnson *Produced by* Jeff Sharp. With Meryl Streep (Lila Ross), Claire Danes (Ann Grant), Mamie Gummer (Lila Wittenborn), Toni Collette (Nina Mars), Vanessa Redgrave (Ann Lord), Patrick Wilson (Harris Arden), Hugh Dancy (Buddy Wittenborn), Natasha Richardson (Constance Haveford).

Rendition
Directed by Gavin Hood *Screenplay* Kelley Sane *Cinematography* Dion Beebe *Set Decoration* Jille Azis *Original Music* Paul Hepker and Mark Kilian *Film Editing* Megan Gill *Produced by* Steve Golin and Marcus Viscidi. With Meryl Streep (Corrine Whitman), Jake Gyllenhaal (Douglas Freeman), Reese Witherspoon (Isabella Fields El-Ibrahimi), Alan Arkin (Senator Hawkins), Peter Sarsgaard (Alan Smith), Omar Metwally (Anwar El-Ibrahimi).

Lions for Lambs
Directed by Robert Redford *Screenplay* Matthew Michael Carnahan *Cinematography* Philippe Rousselot *Set Decoration* Leslie A. Pope *Original Music* Mark Isham *Film Editing* Joe Hutshing *Produced by* Matthew Michael Carnahan, Tracy Falco, Andrew Hauptman, and Robert Redford. With Meryl Streep (Janine Roth), Robert Redford (Professor Stephen Malley), Tom Cruise (Senator Jasper Irving), Michael Peña (Ernest Rodriguez), Andrew Garfield (Todd Hayes).

2008
Mamma Mia!
Directed by Phyllida Lloyd *Screenplay* Catherine Johnson, based on her musical with songs by ABBA *Cinematography* Haris Zambarloukos *Set Decoration* Barbara Herman-Skelding *Original Music* Benny Andersson *Film Editing* Lesley Walker *Produced by* Judy Craymer and Gary Goetzman. With Meryl Streep (Donna), Pierce Brosnan (Sam), Colin Firth (Harry), Stellan Skarsgard (Bill), Julie Walters (Rosie), Amanda Seyfried (Sophie), Christine Baranski (Tanya).

Doubt
Directed by John Patrick Shanley *Screenplay* John Patrick Shanley, based on his play *Cinematography* Roger Deakins *Set Decoration* Ellen Christiansen *Original Music* Howard Shore *Film Editing* Dylan Tichenor *Produced by* Mark Roybal and Scott Rudin. With Meryl Streep (Sister Aloysius Beauvier), Philip Seymour Hoffman (Father Brendan Flynn), Amy Adams (Sister James), Viola Davis (Mrs. Miller), Alice Drummond (Sister Veronica), Susan Blommaert (Mrs. Carson).

2009
Julie & Julia
Directed by Nora Ephron *Screenplay* Nora Ephron, based on a book by Julie Powell and on a book by Julia Child and Alex Prud'homme *Cinematography* Stephen Goldblatt *Set Decoration* Susan Bode *Original Music* Alexandre Desplat *Film Editing* Richard Marks *Produced by* Nora Ephron, Laurence Mark, Amy Robinson, and Eric Steel. With Meryl Streep (Julia Child), Amy Adams (Julie Powell), Stanley Tucci (Paul Child), Chris Messina (Eric Powell), Linda Emond (Simone Beck), Helen Carey (Louisette Bertholle).

It's Complicated
Directed by Nancy Meyers *Screenplay* Nancy Meyers *Cinematography* John Toll *Set Decoration* Beth A. Rubino *Original Music* Heitor Pereira and Hans Zimmer *Film Editing* Joe Hutshing and David Moritz *Produced by* Nancy Meyers and Scott Rudin. With Meryl Streep (Jane Adler), Steve Martin (Adam Schaffer), Alec Baldwin (Jake Adler), John Krasinski (Harley), Lake Bell (Agness Adler), Rita Wilson (Trisha).

2010
Web Therapy (Online series)
"Camilly Bowner: Aversion Therapy" (Season 3, Episode 16, November 8, 2010)
"Camilly Bowner: Healing Touch" (Season 3, Episode 17, November 11, 2010)
"Camilly Bowner: Reverse Psychology" (Season 3, Episode 18, November 13, 2010)
Directed by Don Roos *Screenplay* Lisa Kudrow, Dan Bucantinsky, and Don Roos *Cinematography* Michael Goi *Film Editing* David Codron *Produced by* Jodi Binstock. With Meryl Streep (Camilla Bowner), Lisa Kudrow (Fiona Wallice).

2011
The Iron Lady
Directed by Phyllida Lloyd *Screenplay* Abi Morgan *Cinematography* Elliot Davis *Set Decoration* Annie Gilhooly *Original Music* Thomas Newman *Film Editing* Justine Wright *Produced by* Damian Jones. With Meryl Streep (Margaret Thatcher), Jim Broadbent (Denis Thatcher), Olivia Colman (Carol Thatcher), Anthony Head (Geoffrey Howe), Iain Glen (Alfred Roberts), Alexandra Roach (Young Margaret Thatcher), Harry Lloyd (Young Denis Thatcher).

2012
Hope Springs
Directed by David Frankel *Screenplay* Vanessa Taylor *Cinematography* Florian Ballhaus *Set Decoration* George DeTitta Jr. *Original Music* Theodore Shapiro *Film Editing* Steven Weisberg *Produced by* Todd Black and Guymon Casady. With Meryl Streep (Kay Soames), Tommy Lee Jones (Arnold Soames), Steve Carell (Dr. Feld), Jean Smart (Eileen), Ben Rappaport (Brad), Marin Ireland (Molly).

2013
August: Osage County
Directed by John Wells *Screenplay* Tracy Letts, based on her play *Cinematography* Adriano Goldma *Set Decoration* Nancy Haigh *Film Editing* Stephen Mirrione *Produced by* George Clooney, Jean Doumanian, Grant Heslov, Steve Traxler, and Harvey Weinstein. With Meryl Streep (Violet Weston), Sam Shepard (Beverly Weston), Julia Roberts (Barbara Weston Fordham), Benedict Cumberbatch ("Little" Charles Aiken), Margo Martindale (Mattie Fae Aiken), Ewan McGregor (Bill Fordham), Abigail Breslin (Jean Fordham).

The Homesman
Directed by Tommy Lee Jones *Screenplay* Tommy Lee Jones, based on a novel by Glendon Swarthout *Cinematography* Rodrigo Prieto *Set Decoration* Wendy Ozols-Barnes *Original Music* Marco Beltrami *Film Editing* Roberto Silvi *Produced by* Luc Besson, Peter Brant, Michael Fitzgerald, Tommy Lee Jones, and Brian Kennedy. With Meryl Streep (Altha Carter), Tommy Lee Jones (George Briggs), Hilary Swank (Mary Bee Cuddy), Grace Gummer (Arabella Sours), Miranda Otto (Theoline Belknapp), Sonja Richter (Gro Svendsen).

Bibliography

Books

Rachel Abramowitz, *Is That a Gun In Your Pocket?: Women's Experience of Power in Hollywood*, Random House, 2000.
Karen Hollinger, *The Actress: Hollywood Acting and the Female Star*, Routledge, 2006.

Articles

Emma Brockes, "The Devil in Ms. Streep," *The Guardian*, September 22, 2006.
Brad Darrach, "Meryl Streep on Top—and Tough Enough to Stay There," *Life*, December 1987.
Lawrence Grobel, "Meryl Streep: A Tough Act to Follow," *Movieline*, August 1, 1992.
Mel Gussow, "The Rising Star of Meryl Streep," *The New York Times Magazine*, February 14, 1979.
Mark Harris, "Depth Becomes Her," *Entertainment Weekly*, March 24, 2000.
Molly Haskell, "Hiding in the Spotlight," *Ms.*, December 1988.
Bernard Weinraub, "Her Peculiar Career; Meryl Streep," *The New York Times*, September 8, 1994.
Vicki Woods, "Meryl Streep: Force of Nature," *Vogue*, January 2012.

Radio, TV and Film

Meryl Streep: The Fresh Air Interview, National Public Radio, February 6, 2012.
"Meryl Streep," *Inside the Actors Studio*, Bravo TV, November 22, 1998.

1　Meryl Streep, commencement speech at Barnard College, New York, May 17, 2010.

2　Terry Gross and Meryl Streep, *Meryl Streep: The Fresh Air Interview*, National Public Radio, February 6, 2012. Accessible at http://www.npr.org/2012/02/06/146362798/meryl-streep-the-fresh-air-interview.

3　*Ibid.*

4　*Ibid.*

5　Meryl Streep, Barnard, *op. cit.*

6　*Fresh Air*, *op. cit.*

7　*Ibid.*

8　Jennifer Greenstein Altmann, "Meryl Streep Talks About the 'Mysterious' Art of Acting," *News at Princeton*, December 1, 2006. Accessible at www.princeton.edu/main/news/archive/S16/49/92S82/.

9　Commencement address Meryl Streep delivered to graduating Vassar class of 1983.

10　*Fresh Air*, *op. cit.*

11　David Rosenthal, "Meryl Streep Stepping In and Out of Roles," *Rolling Stone*, October 15, 1981.

12　Mel Gussow, "The Rising Star of Meryl Streep," *The New York Times Magazine*, February 4, 1979.

13　Bob Greene, "Streep," *Esquire*, December 1984.

14　*Ibid.*

15　"Meryl Streep," *Inside the Actors Studio*, Bravo TV, November 22, 1998.

16　Mel Gussow, *op. cit.*

17　Transcript of the Hollywood Foreign Press Association press conference, October 21, 1988.

18　"Biography: The 1970s," www.simplystreep.com. Accessible at www.simplystreep.com/content/information/biography/bio002.html.

19　Jeff Rovin, "Thoroughly Modern Meryl," *Ladies' Home Journal*, August 1986.

20　Susan Dworkin, "Meryl Streep to the Rescue," *Ms.*, February 1979.

21　*Inside the Actors Studio*, *op. cit.*

22　Mel Gussow, *op. cit.*

23　Brad Darrach, "Meryl Streep on Top—and Tough Enough to Stay There," *Life*, December 1987.

24　*Fresh Air*, *op. cit.*

25　Charles Champlin, "Just an Ordinary Connecticut Housewife," *Los Angeles Times*, November 6, 1988.

26　Richard Schickel, "The Cowboy and the Lady," *Time*, June 5, 1995.

27　Leslie Bennetts, "Something About Meryl," *Vanity Fair*, January 2010.

28　Jennifer Greenstein Altmann, *op. cit.*

29　Scott Brown, "Streep at the Top," *The Hollywood Reporter*, November 1983.

30　Jennifer Greenstein Altmann, *op. cit.*

31　Vicki Woods, "Meryl Streep: Force of Nature," *Vogue*, January 2012.

32　*Ibid.*

33　Karen Hollinger, *The Actress: Hollywood Acting and the Female Star*, Routledge, 2006, p. 95.

34　Molly Haskell, "Hiding in the Spotlight," *Ms.*, December 1988.

35　Roger Copeland, "A Vietnam Movie That Does Not Knock America," *The New York Times*, August 7, 1977.

36　Michael Deeley, *Blade Runners, Deer Hunters & Blowing the Bloody Doors Off: My Life in Cult Movies*, Faber & Faber, 2008, p. 131.

37　Michael Deeley, *op. cit.*, p. 169.

38　No byline, Meryl Streep interviewed in *Hello!*, May 7, 2012.

39　Mel Gussow, *op. cit.*

40　Scot Haller, "Star Treks: Four Distinctive Young Stage Actresses Arrive at Coast-to-Coast Visibility," *Horizon*, August 1978.

41　Susan Dworkin, *op. cit.*

42　Mel Gussow, *op. cit.*

43　Susan Dworkin, *op. cit.*

44　Meryl Streep, Barnard, *op. cit.*

45　*The Deer Hunter* Press Notes, Universal Pictures publicity.

46　Corby Kummer, "Streep vs. Streep," *Cue*, January 5, 1979.

47　Richard Shepard, *I Knew It Was You: Rediscovering John Cazale*, HBO Films, 2009.

48　Rachel Abramowitz, "Streep Fighter," *Premiere* (UK), June 1997.

49　Roger Copeland, *op. cit.*

50　*The Deer Hunter* Press Notes, *op. cit.*

51　Robert Hofler, *Party Animals: A Hollywood Tale of Sex, Drugs, and Rock 'n' Roll, Starring the Fabulous Allan Carr*, De Capo Press, 2010, p. 87.

52　Pauline Kael, "The God-Bless-America Symphony," *The New Yorker*, December 18, 1978.

53　Bill Krohn, "Interview with Michael Cimino," *Cahiers du cinéma*, June 1982.

54　Lee Grant, "Controversy, Glitter, War and Peace at the Awards," *Los Angeles Times*, April 11, 1979.

55　*Ibid.*

56　David Denby, "The Movie Slayers," *New York*, June 18, 1979.

57　Lawrence Grobel, "Meryl Streep: A Tough Act to Follow," *Movieline*, August 1, 1992.

58　Mark Harris, "Depth Becomes Her," *Entertainment Weekly*, March 24, 2000.

59　Susan Dworkin, *op. cit.*

60　*Ibid.*

61　Jack Kroll, "A Star for the '80s," *Newsweek*, January 1980.

62　No byline, "Hollywood Finds a Refreshing '79-Style Golden Girl Who Insists on Being Her Own Woman,"

People, December 24, 1979.

63 *Kramer vs. Kramer* Production Notes, Columbia Pictures.

64 Janet Maslin, "Meryl Streep Pauses for Family Matters," *The New York Times*, August 24, 1979.

65 *Ibid.*

66 Gerald Clarke, "A Father Finds His Son," *Time*, December 3, 1979.

67 Corby Kummer, *op. cit.*

68 Corby Kummer, *op. cit.*

69 Emma Brockes, "The Devil in Ms. Streep," *The Guardian*, September 22, 2006.

70 Rachel Abramowitz, *Is That a Gun in Your Pocket?: Women's Experience of Power in Hollywood*, Random House, 2000, p. 129.

71 Susan Dworkin, *op. cit.*

72 Lawrence Grobel, *op. cit.*

73 Jack Kroll, *op. cit.*

74 Bruce Kirkland, "Fatherly Love," *Marquee*, November/December, 1979.

75 Paul Gray, "A Mother Finds Herself," *Time*, December 3, 1979.

76 Jack Kroll, *op. cit.*

77 *Kramer vs. Kramer* Production Notes, *op. cit.*

78 "The Myth of Equal Rights Amendment April 29, 1979," Ford Hall Forum at Suffolk University. Accessible at www.fordhallforum.org/ archives/04-29-1979.

79 Frank Rich, "Grownups, A Child, Divorce, and Tears," *Time*, December 3, 1979.

80 Michael Sragow, "Breaking Up Is So Hard to Do," *Los Angeles Herald Examiner*, December 16, 1979.

81 Stephen Farber, "Bringing Up Daddy," *New West*, December 17, 1979.

82 Gregg Kilday, "Kramer Wins Big in the Highest Court," *Los Angeles Herald Examiner*, April 15, 1980.

83 Ralph Kaminsky, "Kramer Winners Transform Traditional Oscar Interviews," *Boxoffice*, April 21, 1980. Account of the scene backstage at the Oscars also pulls from Gregg Kilday, *op. cit.*

84 Peter J. Boyer, "Streep: A Reluctant Passenger on the Hoopla Express," *Los Angeles Times*, September 20, 1981.

85 Diane De Dubovay, "I Don't Want to Be a Superstar," *Woman's Day*, March 1980.

86 *Ibid.*

87 David Lewin, "The Magic of Meryl," *New Idea*, March 1983.

88 William Wolf, "Meryl Streep, Kevin Kline," *Moviegoer*, January 1983.

89 Jack Kroll, *op. cit.*

90 John Skow, "What Makes Meryl Magic," *Time*, September 7, 1981.

91 William Wolf, *op. cit.*

92 Corby Kummer, *op. cit.*

93 David Rosenthal, *op. cit.*

94 John Skow, *op. cit.*

95 William Wolf, *op. cit.*

96 Joan Goodman, "Streep's Choice," *You*, April 1983.

97 William Wolf, *op. cit.*

98 Charles Champlin, "Streep's Sophie: An Amazement," *Los Angeles Times*, December 11, 1982.

99 *Death Dreams of Mourning* by director Charles Kiselyak, special feature on *Sophie's Choice* DVD, produced in 1997.

100 John Skow, *op. cit.*

101 Joan Goodman, *op. cit.*

102 *Theater of War* by director John Walter, Alive Mind, 2008.

103 Joan Goodman, *op. cit.*

104 Charles Champlin, "*Sophie's*—on Location in Flatbush," *Los Angeles Times*, May 16, 1982.

105 Director's commentary track on *Sophie's Choice* DVD, released April 21, 1998, by Lions Gate Home Entertainment.

106 William Wolf, *op. cit.*

107 *Ibid.*

108 *Ibid.*

109 Director's commentary track on *Sophie's Choice* DVD, *op. cit.*

110 *Ibid.*

111 *Ibid.*

112 *Ibid.*

113 *Death Dreams of Mourning*, *op. cit.*

114 *Sophie's Choice* director's commentary, *op. cit.*

115 Roderick Mann, "Great Diet," *Los Angeles Times*, April 19, 1983.

116 *Death Dreams of Mourning*, *op. cit.*

117 *Ibid.*

118 Mel Gussow, *op. cit.*

119 Peter Travers and Carol Wallace, "Oscar: And the Winner Is…," *People*, April 4, 1983.

120 No byline, "Film Review: Sophie's Choice," *Variety*, December 7, 1982.

121 Peter Rainer, "Except for Streep, 'Sophie's' Not Choice," *Los Angeles Herald Examiner*, December 10, 1982.

122 Joy Gould Boyum, "Formidable Performances by Streep and Newman," *The Wall Street Journal*, December 10 1982.

123 Pauline Kael, "Tootsie, Gandhi, and Sophie," *The New Yorker*, December 27, 1982.

124 Stuart Jeffries, "A Legend Lightens Up," *The Guardian*, July 1, 2008.

125 Academy of Motion Picture Arts and Sciences, "Meryl Streep Winning an Oscar® for 'Sophie's Choice'". Accessible on YouTube.

126 Robert Pace, "Oscars Flashback '83: Pregnant Meryl Wins Actress," *Entertainment Tonight*, November 5, 2012. Accessible at http://www.etonline.com/awards/oscars/126518_Oscars_Flashback_Meryl_Streep_1983/index.html.

127 Roger Ebert, *Awake in the Dark: The Best of Roger Ebert*, University of Chicago Press, 2008, p. 67.

128 Joyce Egginton, "The Karen Silkwood File," *The Observer*, April 6, 1984.

129 *Ibid.*

130 Thomas Wiener, "Meryl Streep on Silkwood: She Wasn't a Saint," *Los Angeles Herald Examiner*, December 15, 1983.

131 Roger Ebert, *op. cit.*, p. 65.

132 Andrew Laskos, "The Detour in the Path of *Silkwood*," *Los Angeles Times*, April 10, 1977.

133 Andrew Kurtzman, "The Struggle to Film *Silkwood*," *The Village Voice*, December 20, 1983.

134 Joyce Egginton, *op. cit.*

135 Thomas Wiener, *op. cit.*

136 Charles Champlin, "Meryl Streep as Silkwood and Herself," *Los Angeles Times*, December 18, 1983.

137 *Ibid.*

138 *Ibid.*

139 David Rosenthal, *op. cit.*

140 Diana Maychick, *Meryl Streep: The Reluctant Superstar*, St. Martin's Press, 1984, p. 143.

141 Diana Maychick, *op. cit.*, p. 144.

142 Thomas Wiener, *op. cit.*

143 Brad Darrach, *op. cit.*

144 Roger Ebert, *op. cit.*, p. 67.

145 George Anthony, "A Conversation with a Natural Actress," *Marquee*, December 1983.

146 Roger Ebert, *op. cit.*, p. 66.

147 Susan King, "Director Mike Nichols on his Actors," *Los Angeles Times*, June 9, 2010.

148 Roger Ebert, *op. cit.*, p. 64.

149 Joyce Egginton, *op. cit.*

150 George Anthony, *op. cit.*

151 Jay Carr, "Women Are Getting a Fairer Shake," *Los Angeles Times*, December 30, 1983.

152 Patrick McGilligan, *Backstory 5: Interviews with Screenwriters of the 1990s*, University of California Press, 2010.

153 Stephen Schiff, "Seeing the Light," *Vanity Fair*, February 1984.

154 Jack Kroll, "Deadly Grievances," *Newsweek*, December 12, 1983.

155 James Wolcott, "Silkwood's Blight," *Texas Monthly*, February 1984.

156 Pauline Kael, "Silkwood," *The New Yorker*, January 9, 1984.

157 Peter Carlson, "*Silkwood*'s Real-Life Characters Find Much to Praise—And A Few Inaccuracies—in the Hit Film," *People*, February 20, 1984.

158 *Ibid.*

159 Joyce Egginton, *op. cit.*

160 "Mike Nichols in Conversation" at the Museum of Modern Art in New York, April 18, 2009. Accessible at http://www.moma.org/explore/multimedia/videos/34/263.

161 George Hadley Garcia, "Streep's Ahead," *Photoplay*, November 1985.

162 Carol Wallace, "Streep and Redford Battle Lions, Snakes, Storms and Controversy to Bring *Out of Africa* to the Screen," *People*, January 20, 1986.

163 Michael Feeney Callan, *Robert Redford: The Biography*, Alfred A. Knopf, 2011, p. 365.

164 *A Song of Africa*, by director Charles Kiselyak, extra content on *Out of Africa* DVD, released by Universal Pictures, 2000.

165 Brad Darrach, *op. cit.*

166 Digby Diehl, "To Sydney Pollack Every Movie Can Be a Love Story," *Los Angeles Herald Examiner*, March 16, 1986.

167 David Denby, "Redford Hunts Streep in *Out of Africa*," *New York*, September 16, 1985.

168 Digby Diehl, *op. cit.*

169 Digby Diehl, "Dinesen's Biographer-Turned-Filmmaker," *Los Angeles Herald Examiner*, January 29, 1986.

170 *A Song of Africa*, *op. cit.*

171 Rick Lyman, "Literary Classic Finally Comes to the Screen," *Press-Telegram*, December 25, 1985.

172 Emma Brockes, *op. cit.*

173 Michael Feeney Callan, *op. cit.*, p. 300.

174 *Ibid.*

175 Carol Wallace, *op. cit.*

176 Kathy Eldon, "Exclusive Report: Redford and Streep in Kenya," *Playgirl*, January 1986.

177 Michael Feeney Callan, *op. cit.*, p. 364.

178 Cyndi Stivers, "Class Project: The Making of *Out of Africa*," *Us*, January 27, 1986.

179 Michael Feeney Callan, *op. cit.*, p. 298.

180 Michael Feeney Callan, *op. cit.*, p. 367.

181 Bart Mills, "Out of Africa," *Movieland*, February 1986.

182 *Ibid.*

183 Wendy Wasserstein, "Streeping Beauty," *Interview*, December 1988.

184 *Inside the Actors Studio*, *op. cit.*

185 Stanley Kauffmann, "The African Queen," *The New Republic*, January 20, 1986.

186 Gene Siskel, "Meryl Streep Not Looking for a Role as an American Icon," *Chicago Tribune*, July 20, 1986.

187 Damien Bona and Mason Wiley, *Inside Oscar: The Unofficial History of the Academy Awards*, Ballantine Books, 1996, p. 665.

188 Pauline Kael, "Sacred Monsters," *The New Yorker*, December 30, 1985.

189 Molly Haskell, "Out of Dinesen," *Ms.*, March 1986.

190 Brad Darrach, *op. cit.*

191 David Handelman, "Winning Streep," *Vogue*, April 1992.

192 Teresa Carpenter, "Hope I Die Before I Get Old," *Premiere*, September 1992.

193 Vicki Woods, *op. cit.*

194 Mike Hammer, "Is Meryl Streep Ever Going to Lighten Up?" *Sunday Star*, October 23, 1988.

195 Nina J. Easton, "Meryl Streep's Latest Accent Is a Laugh," *Los Angeles Times*, December 10, 1989.

196 Joy Horowitz, "That Madcap Meryl. Really!" *The New York Times*, March 17, 1991.

197 Nina J. Easton, *op. cit.*

198 Hilary de Vries, "Meryl Acts Up," *Los Angeles Times*, September 9, 1990.

199 Nina J. Easton, *op. cit.*

200 *Fresh Air*, *op. cit.*

201 Frank Sanello, "Meryl Streep in New Film," *Rome News-Tribune*, September 7, 1990.

202 Glenn Plaskin, "Meryl Streep's Focus Is Work; Private Life Is Not for Sale," *The Seattle Times*, September 21, 1990.

203 Liz Smith, "Streep's Losing Streak," *Los Angeles Times*, May 20, 1991.

204 *Death Becomes Her* Production Notes, Universal Studios Press Department.

205 Mark Harris, *op. cit.*

206 David Handelman, *op. cit.*

207 Teresa Carpenter, *op. cit.*

208 David Handelman, *op. cit.*

209 *Ibid.*

210 Mark Harris, *op. cit.*

211 Kevin H. Martin, "Life Everlasting," *Cinefex*, November 1992.

212 Teresa Carpenter, *op. cit.*

213 Kevin H. Martin, *op. cit.*

214 Teresa Carpenter, *op. cit.*

215 Geoff Andrew, "Streep Talking," *Time Out London*, November 25, 1992.

216 Mark Harris, *op. cit.*

217 Richard Corliss, "Beverly Hills Corpse," *Time*, August 3, 1992.

218 Ella Taylor, "Return of the She-devils," *LA Weekly*, July 31, 1992.

219 Bernard Weinraub, "Her Peculiar Career; Meryl Streep," *The New York Times*, September 8, 1994.

220 *Ibid.*

221 Lawrence Grobel, *op. cit.*

222 Rachel Abramowitz, 2000, *op. cit.*, p. 339.

223 Brian Case, "Hidden Depths," *Time Out London*, February 22, 1995.

224 Bernard Weinraub, *op. cit.*

225 No byline, "Streep Shoots the Rapids," *Newsweek*, September 25, 1994.

226 Rachel Abramowitz, 2000, *op. cit.*, p. 413.

227 Bernard Weinraub, *op. cit.*

228 James Greenberg, "The Perils of Meryl," *Entertainment Weekly*, October 7, 1994.

229 Richard Schickel, *op. cit.*

230 Michael Henry Wilson, *Eastwood on Eastwood*, Cahiers du cinéma, 2010.

231 Sean Mitchell, "Clint, By Candlelight," *Los Angeles Times*,

May 28, 1995.

232 Claudia Glenn Dowling, "Madison County Confidential," *Life*, June 1995.

233 Donald Chase, "The Real Meryl Streep Finally Stands Up," *A&E Monthly*, November 1995.

234 Betty Goodwin, "A Model of Simplicity," *Los Angeles Times*, June 1, 1995.

235 *The Bridges of Madison County* Production Notes, Warner Brothers.

236 Claudia Glenn Dowling, *op. cit.*

237 Sean Mitchell, *op. cit.*

238 Richard Schickel, *op. cit.*

239 *The Bridges of Madison County* Production Notes, *op. cit.*

240 Robert E. Kapsis and Kathie Coblentz, *Clint Eastwood: Interviews*, University Press of Mississippi, 1999, p. 236.

241 *The Bridges of Madison County* Production Notes, *op. cit.*

242 Robert E. Kapsis and Kathie Coblentz, *op. cit.*

243 Sean Mitchell, *op. cit.*

244 *Ibid.*

245 Brad Darrach, *op. cit.*

246 James Greenberg, *op. cit.*

247 John Powers, "Bodice Rippers," *Vogue*, July 1995.

248 Ella Taylor, "The Bridges of Madison County," *LA Weekly*, June 2, 1995.

249 Army Archerd, "Just for Variety," *Variety*, June 1, 1995.

250 Janice Page, "Straight Up Streep," *The Boston Globe*, April 2, 2006.

251 Jesse Green, "What, Meryl Worry?" *The New York Times*, July 25, 2004.

252 *Ibid.*

253 Dennis Lim, "Under the Guise of Ingenuity," *Los Angeles Times*, December 10, 2006.

254 Karen Hollinger, *op. cit.*, p. 79.

255 Kevin West, "Two Queens," *W*, May 2006.

256 A. O. Scott, "Sadistic, Manipulative and So Very Stylish," *The New York Times*, June 30, 2006.

257 Kevin West, *op. cit.*

258 No byline, "*Elle* Asks Meryl Streep…," *Elle* (UK), November 2006.

259 Emma Brockes, *op. cit.*

260 Anne Thompson, "Drama Queen," *The Hollywood Reporter*, December 2006.

261 Karen Idelson, "Meryl Streep, 'The Devil Wears Prada,'" *Variety*, December 13, 2006.

262 Emma Brockes, *op. cit.*

263 *The Devil Wears Prada* Press Kit, 20th Century Fox.

264 Kevin West, *op. cit.*

265 Belinda Luscombe, "7 Myths About Meryl," *Time*, June 11, 2006.

266 *Devil* Press Kit, *op. cit.*

267 Robert Hofler, "Meryl as Co-star and Coach," *Variety*, April 14, 2008.

268 Karen Idelson, *op. cit.*

269 Emma Brockes, *op. cit.*

270 Robert Hofler, 2008, *op. cit.*

271 Karen Idelson, *op. cit.*

272 Anne Thompson, "Exec with Character Does Films with Same," *The Hollywood Reporter*, June 30, 2006.

273 Clark Collis, "Silver Streak," *Entertainment Weekly*, January 19, 2007.

274 Anne Thompson, December 2006, *op. cit.*

275 Rachel Abramowitz, "She Has to Laugh," *Los Angeles Times*, November 30, 2008.

276 *Ibid.*

277 Nicole LaPorte and Gabriel Snyder, "Auds Dance with 'The Devil,'" *Variety*, July 10, 2006.

278 Mark Feeney, "Hail to the Streep," *The Boston Globe*, July 25, 2004.

279 Dennis Lim, *op. cit.*

280 Carina Chocano, "The Mark of a Pro," *Los Angeles Times*, January 31, 2007.

281 Ella Taylor, "En Vogue," *LA Weekly*, June 30, 2006.

282 Peter Bart, "Blindsided by 'Borat' and 'The Devil,'" *Variety*, November 13, 2006.

283 Peter Travers, "Meryl Streep," *Rolling Stone*, November 15, 2007.

284 *Fresh Air*, *op. cit.*

285 *Fresh Air*, *op. cit.*

286 Martyn Palmer, "Meryl Streep Up Close," *Good Housekeeping*, August 2008.

287 Leslie Bennetts, *op. cit.*

288 Basinger cited in Rachel Abramowitz, "Meryl Streep's Got Legs," *Los Angeles Times*, September 12, 2009.

289 Leslie Bennetts, *op. cit.*

290 Leslie Bennetts, *op. cit.*

291 Rachel Abramowitz, 2008, *op. cit.*

292 *Ibid.*

293 *Fresh Air*, *op. cit.*

294 Leslie Bennetts, *op. cit.*

295 Mark Feeney, *op. cit.*

296 Leslie Bennetts, *op. cit.*

297 Anne Thompson, December 2006, *op. cit.*

298 Marisa Fox, "Ladies Who Lunch," *Ladies' Home Journal*, August 2009.

299 Wendy Gordon, "Acting and Activism: Q&A with Meryl Streep," *OnEarth*, February 25, 2012.

300 *Fresh Air*, *op. cit.*

301 Marisa Fox, *op. cit.*

302 *Ibid.*

303 Leslie Bennetts, *op. cit.*

304 *Fresh Air*, *op. cit.*

305 Rachel Abramowitz, 2009, *op. cit.*

306 Marisa Fox, *op. cit.*

307 *Ibid.*

308 *Ibid.*

309 *Ibid.*

310 *Ibid.*

311 Jay A. Fernandez, "She's Really Cooking," *The Hollywood Reporter*, July 31, 2009.

312 A. O. Scott, "That Unmistakable Streepness," *The New York Times*, February 21, 2010.

313 Carrie Rickey, "A Film as Delicious as French Cuisine," *The Philadelphia Inquirer*, August 7, 2009.

314 Dana Stevens, "Julie & Julia," *Slate*, August 6, 2009.

315 Jay A. Fernandez, *op. cit.*

316 Vicki Woods, *op. cit.*

317 Leslie Bennetts, *op. cit.*

318 Rachel Abramowitz, 2009, *op. cit.*

319 Leslie Bennetts, *op. cit.*

320 Peter Travers, *op. cit.*

321 Dennis Lim, *op. cit.*

322 Vicki Woods, *op. cit.*

323 *Ibid.*

324 Gabrielle Donnelly, "With an Oscar Nomination Already in the Cards for Her Portrayal of Margaret Thatcher, Meryl Streep Finds Common Ground with the Iron Lady and Remembers Her Nerves at Taking on a British Icon." *Hello!* (UK), January 8, 2012.

325 *Fresh Air*, *op. cit.*

326 *Ibid.*

327 *Ibid.*

328 *Ibid.*

329 Rebecca Keegan, "Two 'Iron' Wills," *Los Angeles Times*, February 7, 2012.

330 *Fresh Air*, *op. cit.*

331 Vicki Woods, *op. cit.*

332 Gabriella Donnelly, *op. cit.*

333 Vicki Woods, *op. cit.*

334 Pamela McClintock, "Oscar Nominee Meryl Streep Says Thatcher Was a Feminist," *The Hollywood Reporter*, February 14, 2012.

335 Gabriella Donnelly, *op. cit.*

336 Vicki Woods, *op. cit.*

337 Simon Walters, "Friends Revulsion at Film That Portrays Lady Thatcher as 'Granny Going Mad,'" *Daily Mail*, August 20, 2011.

338 Rebecca Keegan, *op. cit.*

339 Betsy Sharkey, "Softened by Time," *Los Angeles Times*, December 30, 2011.

340 Charles McNulty, "Critic's Notebook: My Meryl Streep Problem," *Los Angeles Times*, February 26, 2012.

341 Wendy Wasserstein, *op. cit.*

342 Nicole Sperling, "'Iron' Onscreen, Like 'a Kid' Off," *Los Angeles Times*, February 27, 2012.

343 Vicki Woods, *op. cit.*

344 Rebecca Keegan, "Meryl Streep's Next Project: A National Women's History Museum," *Los Angeles Times*, December 28, 2011.

Sidebar Notes

a Scot Haller, *op. cit.*

b *Ibid.*

c Susan Dworkin, *op. cit.*

d Tony Sherman, "*Holocaust* Survivor Shoots *Deer Hunter*, Shuns Fame," *Feature Magazine*, February 1979.

e Frank Rich, "Meryl Streep Sings in 'Alice in Concert,'" *The New York Times*, January 8, 1981.

f Ben Brantley, "THEATER REVIEW; Streep Meets Chekhov, Up in Central Park," *The New York Times*, August 13, 2001.

g Michael Feingold, "Gull Talk," *The Village Voice*, August 14, 2001.

h Hilton Als, "Wagon Train," *The New Yorker*, September 4, 2006.

i *Theater of War*, *op. cit.*

j Pauline Kael, *op. cit.*

k Wendy Wasserstein, "Streeping Beauty," *Interview*, December 1988.

l Brad Darrach, *op. cit.*

m *Ibid.*

n "Mike Nichols Salutes Meryl Streep at AFI Life Achievement Award," YouTube, uploaded April 7, 2009. Accessible at http://www.youtube.com/watch?v=2coyhd_pXy8.

o Bernard Weinraub, *op. cit.*

p "Episode 4: Know Thyself," *Faces of America with Henry Louis Gates, Jr.*, PBS, March 3, 2010.

q George Hadley Garcia, *op. cit.*

r Kathy Eldon, *op. cit.*

s No byline, "Film Clips: Doubles Match," *The Los Angeles Times*, December 11, 1985.

t Molly Haskell, "Finding Herself: The Prime of Meryl Streep," *Film Comment*, May 2008.

u Nina J. Easton, *op. cit.*

v *Ibid.*

w *Ibid.*

x Vincent Canby, "Streep Spars with Barr in a Comedy of Revenge," *The New York Times*, December 8, 1989.

y Ryan Murphy, "Streep Swings from Hysteria to Hysterical," *Press-Telegram*, September 14, 1990.

z Rachel Abramowitz, 2000, *op. cit.*, p. 335.

aa Rachel Abramowitz, 2000, *op. cit.*, p. 335.

bb Amy Dawes, "Screen Seems No Place for Women," *Variety*, August 2, 1990.

cc Ethlie Ann Vare, "Meryl Streep," *The Beat*, May 2, 1991.

dd Rachel Abramowitz, 2000, *op. cit.*, p. 337.

ee James Atlas, "The Glorious Days of Nora Ephron," *Newsweek*, July 9, 2012.

ff *Ibid.*

gg "Nora Ephron Highly Recommends Having Meryl Streep Play You," YouTube, uploaded on April 3, 2009. Accessible at http://www.youtube.com/watch?v=M4Moh-Sw7xE.

hh Frank Rich, "Nora's Secret," *New York*, August 16, 2012.

ii James Atlas, *op. cit.*

jj Peter Knegt, "Jake Gyllenhaal Presents Meryl Streep with Berlinale's Honorary Golden Bear (and Clears Up Some Personal Issues Between Them)," *Indiewire*, February 15, 2012.

kk *Fresh Air*, *op. cit.*

ll David Germain, "Spencer Wins Supporting-Actress Oscar for 'Help,'" Associated Press, February 28, 2012.

mm Rebecca Keegan, *op. cit.*

Original title: *Meryl Streep*
© 2013 Cahiers du cinéma
SARL

Titre original :
Meryl Streep © 2013
Cahiers du cinéma SARL

This Edition published by
Phaidon Press Limited
under licence from Cahiers
du cinéma SARL, 65, rue
Montmartre, 75002 Paris,
France © 2013 Cahiers
du cinéma SARL.

Cette Édition est publiée
par Phaidon Press Limited
avec l'autorisation des
Cahiers du cinéma SARL,
65, rue Montmartre,
75002 Paris, France © 2013
Cahiers du cinéma SARL.

All rights reserved. No part
of this publication may
be reproduced, stored in
a retrieval system or
transmitted, in any form
or by any means, electronic,
mechanical, photocopying,
recording or otherwise,
without the prior permission
of Cahiers du cinéma.

Tous droits réservés.
Aucune partie de cette édition
ne peut être reproduite,
stockée ou diffusée sous
quelque forme que ce soit,
électronique, mécanique,
photocopie, enregistrement,
sans l'autorisation
des Cahiers du cinéma Sarl.

Cahiers du cinéma
65, rue Montmartre
75002 Paris

www.cahiersducinema.com

ISBN 978 0 7148 6669 7

A CIP catalogue record
of this book is available from
the British Library.

Series concept designed
by Thomas Mayfried
Designed by Ron Woods

Printed in China

Photographic credits

ABC Motion Pictures/Twentieth Century
Fox: p. 75; Alan Zanger/© Bettmann/
CORBIS: p. 14; Amblin/Warner Bros.:
p. 123; © Christian Simonpietri/Sygma/
Corbis: p. 51; Collection Archives du 7e
Art/Photo12/Columbia Pictures:
pp. 140, 143, 144-145, 148, 153;
Collection Archives du 7e Art/Photo12/
Pathé International/Alex Bailey:
p. 169; Collection Archives du 7e Art/
Photo12/Universal Pictures: p. 174 (tl);
Collection BFI/Universal Pictures: p. 91;
Collection Cahiers du cinéma/© 2006
Twentieth Century Fox/Barry Wetcher:
pp. 128, 129, 132 (t, b), 138; Collection
Cahiers du cinéma/ABC Motion
Pictures/Twentieth Century Fox:
pp. 66, 72; Collection Cahiers du cinéma/
Cannon Films/Cannon Int./Warner
Bros.: p. 174 (br); Collection Cahiers
du cinéma/Goodspeed Productions:
p. 177 (bl); Collection Cahiers du cinéma/
MGM: p. 177 (tr); Collection Cahiers
du cinéma/Paramount Pictures: pp.
172-173; Collection Cahiers du cinéma/
Pathé International: p. 178 (br); Collection
Cahiers du cinéma/Pathé International/
Alex Bailey: pp. 154, 158, 160, 162,
163 (t, b), 164-165, 166-167; Collection
Cahiers du cinéma/Picturehouse
Entertainment: p. 177 (tl); Collection
Cahiers du cinéma/TriStar Pictures: p. 174
(bl); Collection Cahiers du cinéma/United
Artists: p. 174 (tr); Collection Cahiers
du cinéma/Universal City Studios, Inc./
Neil Leifer : p. 117; Collection Cahiers du
cinéma/Universal Pictures: pp. 11, 17
(t, b), 90, 93, 96, 108, 177 (br); Collection
Cahiers du cinéma/Universal Pictures/
Deana Newcomb: pp. 98 (b), 102 (t, b);
Collection Cahiers du cinéma/Warner
Bros.: p. 119; Collection Cahiers du
cinéma/Warner Bros./Ken Regan:
pp. 112, 113 (b), 118; Collection Cat's/
© 2006 Twentieth Century Fox/Barry
Wetcher: pp. 126, 130-131, 134-135, 139;
Collection Cat's/Universal Pictures:
pp. 103, 107; Collection Cat's/Warner
Bros./Ken Regan: pp. 110, 113 (t);
Collection Christophel/Columbia Pictures:
p. 150; Collection Christophel/HBO:
p. 70; Collection Christophel/Universal
Pictures: p. 95; Collection Christophel/
Warner Bros.: p. 122; Collection
Cinémathèque française/Universal
Pictures: pp. 83, 85, 98 (t), 109; Collection
Margaret Herrick Library/AMPAS/ABC
Motion Pictures/Twentieth Century Fox:
pp. 69, 73, 76-77, 79; Collection Margaret
Herrick Library/AMPAS/Columbia
Pictures: pp. 34, 37 (b); Collection
Margaret Herrick Library/AMPAS/
Twentieth Century Fox: p. 10; Collection
Margaret Herrick Library/AMPAS/United
Artists/Brian Hamill: p. 13; Collection
Margaret Herrick Library/AMPAS/
Universal Pictures: pp. 18, 20 (t, b), 22,
23, 24-25, 27, 28, 29, 30-31, 48, 53, 82;
Collection Margaret Herrick Library/
AMPAS/Universal Pictures/Josh Weiner:
p. 60; Collection Margaret Herrick
Library/AMPAS/Warner Bros./Ken Regan:
p. 125; Collection Photo12/ABC Motion
Pictures/Twentieth Century Fox: p. 64;
Collection Photo12/Columbia Pictures:
pp. 38-39, 47, 50 (t, b); Collection
Photo12/Universal Pictures:
pp. 54-55, 58-59, 80, 84; Collection
Photo12/Warner Bros.: pp. 120-121;
Collection Photofest/ABC Motion
Pictures/Twentieth Century Fox:
p. 71; CollectionPhotofest/ABC Motion
Pictures/Twentieth Century Fox/Zade
Rosenthal: p. 78; Collection Photofest/
Columbia Pictures: p. 37 (t); Collection
Photofest/Columbia Pictures/Holly
Bower: p. 42; Collection Photofest/HBO:
p. 161; Collection Photofest/MGM/UA:
p. 178 (tl); Collection Photofest/NBC: p.
26; Collection Photofest/Orion Pictures:
p. 106; Collection Photofest/Universal
Pictures: pp. 86-87, 104-105; Columbia
Pictures: pp. 40, 142, 147, 149; © Frederic
Ohringer: cover; © Hulton-Deutsch
Collection/CORBIS: p. 15; Martha Swope
© Billy Rose Theatre Division, The New
York Public Library for the Performing
Arts: p. 45; Pathé International: pp. 156,
159; Published in *Vogue* november 1978:
p. 6; Seth Poppel/Yearbook Library: p. 9
(tl, tr, bl, br); The Kobal Collection/
© 1985 Studiocanal Films LTD/Franck
Connor: p. 92; The Kobal Collection/
ABC Motion Pictures/Twentieth Century
Fox: pp. 67, 68; The Kobal Collection/
Columbia Pictures: p. 43; The Kobal
Collection/Universal Pictures: pp. 52, 63
(t, b); Twentieth Century Fox: p. 136,
178 (tr); Universal Pictures: pp. 33, 57,
61, 89, 101; Warner Bros.: pp. 114, 115,
178 (bl).

All reasonable efforts have been made
to trace the copyright holders of the
photographs used in this book.
We apologize to anyone that we were
unable to reach.

Cover illustration
Meryl Streep in the late 1970s.